Fifty Hikes
in Central
New York

Fifty Hikes in Central New York

Hikes and Backpacking Trips
from the Western Adirondacks
to the Finger Lakes

Dr. William P. Ehling

Photographs by the Author

Backcountry Publications
Woodstock,
Vermont

Taughannock Falls

An Invitation to the Reader

Over time trails can be rerouted and signs and landmarks altered. If you find that changes have occurred on the routes described in this book, please let us know so that corrections may be made in future editions. The author and publisher also welcome other comments and suggestions. Address all correspondence to

Editor, *Fifty Hikes*™
Backcountry Publications
P.O. Box 175
Woodstock, Vermont 05091

Library of Congress Cataloging in Publication Data

Ehling, Bill, 1920-
Fifty hikes in central New York.

Bibliography: p.16
1. Hiking—New York (State)—Guide-books. 2. Backpacking—New York (State)—Guide-books. 3. Cross-country skiing—New York (State)—Guide-books. 4. Snowshoes and snowshoeing—New York (State)—Guide-books. 5. New York (State)—Description and travel—1981- —Guide-books. I. Title. II. Title: 50 hikes in central New York.
GV199.42.N65E37 1984 917.47 84-70169
ISBN 0-942440-17-X

Fifth printing, 1992, updated 1989.

Published by Backcountry Publications
A Division of The Countryman Press, Inc.
Woodstock, Vermont 05091

Printed in the United States of America

Text and cover design by Wladislaw Finne
Trail maps drawn by Richard Widhu

To my children, Teresa, James, and Clare. May the accounts herein add to their love of green hills and forest glens and to their joy of hiking their own part of the world.

Acknowledgments

A book like this is made possible by others, those with the foresight and dedication to preserve the land, plant the seedlings that have become today's forests, and construct the footpaths that allow us to walk the hills, glens, and ravines of this region. To all those—the individual trailbuilder, the concerned environmentalist, the official in charge of our public lands—my sincerest thanks. There are many others to whom I am indebted, those who many years ago introduced me to some of the trails covered in this book and those many friends with whom I have hiked throughout Central New York. I am especially grateful to Patricia Peat, who was assigned to me as my editor; her careful reading, her sharp eye for mistakes, and her concern for the smallest detail have been invaluable aids in writing this book. I also thank Olga, with whom I have hiked many of these trails and who shared with me the demands of this book, the frequent discomforts of pesky insects along the trail, but in the final analysis the excitement of still another hike in a new place. Finally, my thanks to the people who made possible what is today the Finger Lakes Trail, one of the most attractive trail systems in New York State, to my friends of the Onondaga Chapter of the Adirondack Mountain Club, and to all the people in the New York State Department of Environmental Conservation who provide vital information and great personal assistance.

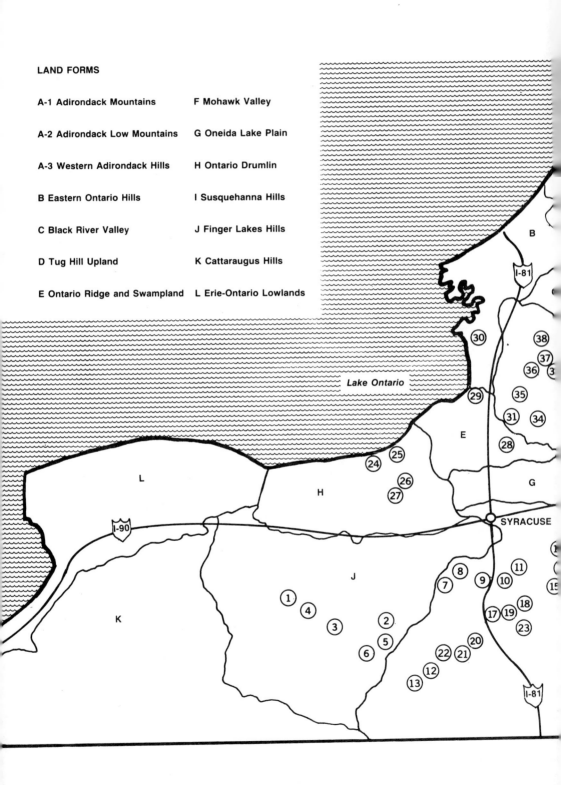

LAND FORMS

A-1 Adirondack Mountains   F Mohawk Valley

A-2 Adirondack Low Mountains   G Oneida Lake Plain

A-3 Western Adirondack Hills   H Ontario Drumlin

B Eastern Ontario Hills   I Susquehanna Hills

C Black River Valley   J Finger Lakes Hills

D Tug Hill Upland   K Cattaraugus Hills

E Ontario Ridge and Swampland   L Erie-Ontario Lowlands

Lake Ontario

SYRACUSE

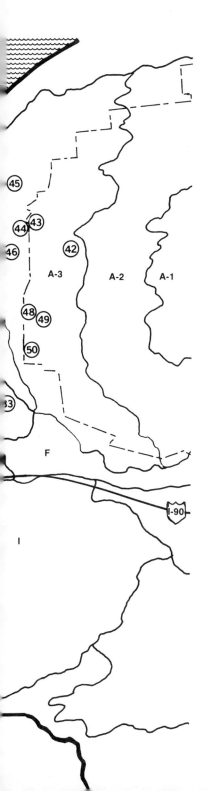

Contents

Tug Hill

Western Adirondack Hills

Introduction

In Central New York, you need never go far to find a marked trail or public land on which to hike. Foot travel in this part of New York is always an adventure, a trek into new places, and hence always a pleasure.

As you hike the many trails of this region, you are struck not only by the area's attractiveness but also by its diversity. While other regions in New York state and throughout the northwest, of course, can make the same claim, it is perhaps the richness of the diversity and the sharp contrasts amid it that somehow set Central New York apart.

There is the varied landscape that ranges from the low, rolling forested hills of the Western Adirondacks in the northeast to wide, sandy beaches found along the east shore of Lake Ontario, and extends from the deep blue waters of the Finger Lakes in the west to the deep, wide valleys in the southeast where the Tioughnioga, Otselic, Chenango, Unadilla, and Susquehanna Rivers flow.

It is a region of prosperous-looking farms and attractive villages, as well as narrow urban corridors running from Herkimer in the east to Rochester in the west in the region's mid-section and from Binghamton in the east to Bath in the west in the region's Southern Tier. It is a place of vineyards and forested hilltops, summer theatres and religious pageants, boat cruises and canoe races, beach resorts and ski centers.

Yet amid all these signs of civilization you find vast tracts of public lands, thick forests, and miles of foot-trails, a quite rural setting that shades into the more rugged grandeur of the backcountry regions where unbroken forests run for miles. Even in a single region, the landscape can prove surprisingly varied. In the flat plain region between Rochester and Syracuse are hundreds of hillocks that mark the presence of hundreds of glacier-produced drumlins, and in the rolling hill country north and south of Syracuse you suddenly encounter breathtakingly deep gorges.

Central New York has a natural richness that you will enjoy in silence and solitude during a day's walk or a weekend outing.

Area and Location. While for those living in the region, Central New York is a well-established geographic entity, the reality may be that Central New York is in part a state of mind. The configuration of the state, which almost resembles a boot, doesn't help matters, nor does the designation of local regions by their own names. Lacking the rectangular shape of, say, Pennsylvania or Massachusetts, New York doesn't allow you easily to mark off an area that can be delimited as "central."

Generally, the land surrounding Syracuse is treated as central, but just how far outward this central region goes is not clear. No matter. For the purpose of this book, the eastern boundary of the territory in which the fifty hiking areas are located can be specified by drawing a line from Potsdam in the north through Herkimer in the Mohawk Valley past the western tip of the Catskill Forest Preserve; this is approximately the same as the 75° longitude line. The boundary on the west is at the 77° 33' longitude mark running south a little to the east of Rochester and through Cohocton in the central area.

In between are the Finger Lakes Region, the elusive central region, the Tug Hill Region, and the Western Adirondack Region—and some of the most scenic landscape in upstate New York.

To put the matter even more simply, all the hiking trails described in this book lie within a 75-mile radius of Syracuse, making it possible to reach every trailhead in about 1½ hours of driving time from there. The region includes 19,000 square miles, including urban and rural areas, farmlands and forestlands, lowlands with elevations of only 260 feet above sea level and highlands with hilltops exceeding 2,000 feet, some of the highest spots west of the high peaks region of the Adirondack Mountains.

Topography and Geology. The topography of this region is shaped by the underlying bedrock and the scouring and erosional action of several continental glaciers that overrode New York state during the Pleistocene period more than 12,000 years ago. It was the glaciers in their forward movement that rounded off the top of hills and mountains and deepened the valleys to give them their unique U-shapes, and it was during deglaciation that glacial meltwaters produced the varied landforms that include gorges, cross-channels, kettle lakes, eskers, kames, plunge pools, valley-head moraines, and outwash plains.

Geologically, four classes of bedrock can be found in this region. In the Western Adirondacks are found igneous and metamorphic rocks, in the Tug Hill region sandstone overlaying shale and shaly

sandstone, and in the central area and the Finger Lakes Region limestone.

Included in this territory are ten different landform regions. South of present-day I-90 (New York State Thruway) are two large regions, roughly divided by I-81 and NY 13 to make up the Susquehanna Hills Region in the east and the Finger Lakes Hills Region in the west. These two regions constitute better than half of the state's Appalachian Uplands—a highland region where hills reach almost 2,000 feet.

North of the Thruway between Rochester and Syracuse is the Ontario Drumlins Region with its countless small hills that look like overturned tea cups or sometimes like loaves of pumpernickel bread.

Immediately east of this region are the Ontario Ridge Swampland Region (encompassing most of Oswego County) and the Oneida Lake Plain Region surrounding Oneida Lake. North of Oneida Lake is the Tug Hill Region, rising ever so steadily from Lake Ontario eastward until it overlooks the Black River Valley from an elevation of 2,200 feet, highest spot west of the Adirondack high peaks. Northwest of Tug Hill is the Eastern Ontario Hills Region, while east of the Black River Valley is the Western Adirondack Hills Region.

These landforms provide a varied landscape that includes a land of low relief bordering Lake Ontario, the sometimes rugged-appearing hill country in the Appalachian highlands, and the dense wilderness-like areas in the central Tug Hill Region and the Western Adirondacks.

Weather and Climate. Central New York's weather can be described as moderate, with warm and usually sunny summers and cold winters marked by predominantly overcast skies. You can expect summer temperatures in the 70s and 80s, while in the winter temperatures will be in the 20s and below. In January and February, cold fronts can send the temperature down to 20 degrees below zero or lower. In general, the mean temperature in January is 20°F; lowland areas average a few degrees higher, while highland areas such as Tug Hill average 15°F.

The mean temperature for July is a comfortable 67°F. Especially in late July and early August, however, temperatures can rise into the low 90s. When the thermometer begins to soar, head for the woods in the highland regions. Hiking forest trails, even on a hot day, can prove surprisingly cool and comfortable.

Average precipitation throughout Central New York is quite uniform, with 2.5 to 3.5 inches falling in every month in most places. Total annual snowfall in and around Syracuse averages in excess of 110 inches for most winters. Because of the "lake effect," that is, conditions produced by air passing over Lake Ontario, the Tug Hill region is the wettest and snowiest in upstate New York; the average snowfall can exceed 250 inches, making this an ideal spot for snowshoeing and cross-country skiing.

Weekend Backpacking and Camping. Virtually all the hiking areas covered in this book lend themselves to weekend backpacking and camping. While most allow camping without permit, a few, such as the Connecticut Hill Wildlife Management Area, require advance permit. These permits can be obtained via telephone or letter from the regional office of the Department of Environmental Conservation (DEC). All such camping-by-permit areas have been noted in the book. In areas where no permit is specified, you may camp for a period of three days. If you plan to stay longer than that, a permit is required.

In a number of areas, especially along the Finger Lakes Trail (FLT), Adirondack-type lean-tos can accommodate hikers and backpackers planning overnight stays. The locations of any lean-tos on the fifty hikes are reported in the book.

Trailheads and Trails. Many of the trailheads of the fifty hikes, while easy to find, have no signs or markers to tell you where the trail begins. Nonetheless, careful reading of the information under the "access" section for each hike should allow you to reach a trailhead without difficulty.

Of the fifty hikes, 27 are on trails that are groomed, marked, and maintained by state, county or federal government agencies or by the Finger Lakes Trail Conference (FLTC). The FLTC, in turn, depends on local hiking groups or individuals to mark and maintain sections of the Finger Lakes Trail, which runs from Allegany State Park in the far southwestern corner of the state across the southern part of the Finger Lakes region to the Catskill Forest Preserve in the east.

The remaining 23 hikes, while they are on public lands, use a trail system that is unmarked; here you walk usually on a combination of dirt roads, truck trails, lanes, and jeep trails. The distinction among these manmade routes is not a sharp one, but there are differences. All truck trails, for example, are dirt roads, but not all dirt roads are truck trails.

Truck trail is a technical designation used by the Department of Environmental Conservation to refer to dirt roads built by the state as access routes to its own land holdings. These are excellent roads, well drained and rarely rutted. They usually are a lane-and-a-half wide (sometimes two) to allow heavy-duty vehicles such as logging trucks to drive into state forests.

Dirt roads off state-owned land are usually county maintained. Lanes, on the other hand, are single-lane roads that, while used by vehicles, are not as a general rule maintained by highway departments; some may be maintained by individual landowners.

The distinction between lane and jeep trail is not sharp. Generally, any road on public lands not publicly maintained is designated as a jeep trail on USGS maps. This refers to a single-lane road, frequently rutted, that can be negotiated only by a four-wheeled drive vehicle.

Ski Touring and Snowshoeing. The hiking areas were picked with an eye to how they lend themselves to such winter activities as ski touring and snowshoeing. With enough snow on the ground, all the trail systems covered in this book can be used by the Nordic skier or snowshoer. Some of them, however, can prove challenging to the ski tourer, demanding the ability of an intermediate or advanced skier. In most cases, though, a novice skier can negotiate the designated trails without too much difficulty.

Some of the hikes in the book are on trail systems especially designed for use by cross-country skiers. This is true of Highland Forest, Chateaugay State Forest, Tug Hill State Forest, Selkirk Shores State Park, and the Lesser Wilderness State Forest. All these trails are marked for skiers, and in the case of Selkirk Shores State Park, the tracks are machine set. The other hiking areas are widely advertised as ski touring areas and attract large numbers of Nordic skiers.

Gear and Clothing. For day hikes in the summer, not much gear is required, but what is, is essential. The most important item is a sturdy day-pack so that you can carry a number of other items that should accompany you on all your hikes, no matter how short.

The "ten essentials" are: (1) food (usually lunch), including such extra ingredients as a meat bar, a tin of pemmican, and a bag of trail mix, say, of raisins, peanuts, chocolate drops and the like; (2) extra clothing, including rain poncho or parka, windbreaker, and/or a wool shirt or sweater; (3) pocket knife with can opener (a Swiss Army knife is a good choice); (4) a plastic bottle with water (don't assume that stream or lake water is safe to drink; it never is); (5) small first aid kit containing aspirin, bandages, moleskin, and first aid cream; (6) pocket-size flashlight; (7) map or maps of the area where you plan to hike; (8) compass; (9) matches in a waterproof container; and (10) firestarters such as candle stubs, fuel tablets, or fire ribbon.

To this list you can add some additional items to make your hiking more enjoyable: insect repellent and sunburn preventive lotion (seasonal), whistle to use if lost, toilet paper, lightweight binoculars, field guides covering items of personal interest such as birds, ferns, flowers, mushrooms and the like, camera and extra film, sunglasses, and a widebrimmed hat to keep the sun off your face, ears, and neck.

Good hiking shoes are a must. Today there are many styles and brands of lightweight boots. Some have an upper portion that is a combination of leather and Gore-Tex; while expensive, they are worth the investment. In any event, the hiking boot ought to be sturdy, about six inches high, with a good sole to give you traction. When buying boots, be sure to try them with the socks you should wear on the trail—a thin inner sock and a thicker, wool outer sock.

In wintertime, of course, extra clothing is required. Dress in the "layering" manner with several layers of clothing that can be removed easily as you begin to perspire; don't wear a single, bulky down jacket, which will cause you to perspire quickly and dampen your inner garments. Footgear also changes in the winter; insulated boots of half-packs are

Old Maple tree seen along trail in Tuller Hill State Forest

necessary if you are hiking in snow or snowshoeing.

Safety and Ethics in the Woods. Compared to the risk involved in driving to the trailhead, hiking in the woods is indeed a safe activity. But mishaps and mistakes can occur—from developing blisters to getting lost. In between there can be such misfortunes as a twisted ankle or a fall resulting in broken bones.

The first step in safety precaution is to plan for the unexpected. This entails becoming familiar with basic first aid. Any course offered by the local chapter of the American Red Cross is a good place to begin. Carry your first aid kit at all times.

Know where you are going. This entails studying your topographical maps covering the area you plan to hike. Always carry a compass, and know how to use map and compass when you reach the trailhead. The best rule to follow is to never walk alone. At the very least, hike with a partner, but the ideal hiking group numbers three people. If anything happens to a group member, one person can search for help, leaving another to stay with the injured and stricken person.

As more people take up hiking and head into the back country, hiking ethics become increasingly important. Whatever you pack in, also pack out; this includes plastic containers, tin cans, wrappers, and the like. The outdoors is not a place to drop your litter. Leave the hiking trail cleaner after you leave than when you begin. This means that if you find litter, pick it up and carry it out.

If you plan to spend a weekend tenting, camp at designated areas or in places where your campsite leaves no trace. Pitch your tent away from water, trailsides, and trailheads. For human waste, find a leaf-covered area or one with soft ground where a suitable hole can be dug. Make sure you are at least 200 feet away from water and from a trail or path.

Don't bathe with soap in lakes or streams, and carry your washwater and dishwater away from the shores. If you plan to camp out, bring a good cook stove; don't try to cook on an open fire. Today's hiking ethic calls for as little use of open fires as possible. If you need a fire, use only deadfall and downed branches. Don't chop down trees.

Clean up your camp site. Try to make the area appear as if no one had tented. Don't bury your trash; pack it out. Finally, respect the rights of others, including the property rights of private landowners and the privacy of fellow hikers.

Distance, Walking Time, and Vertical Rise. At the beginning of each hike, you'll find a summary, listing total hiking distance, hiking time, vertical rise, and map(s).

Total hiking distance includes a round-trip or circuit unless otherwise indicated, with measurements made on a USGS topo map. Such distance measures are given in miles or in some fraction of a mile. Most people who are in good shape and sound health usually can hike up to six miles without experiencing any discomfort either during or after the hike. Most of the hikes in this book fall within this range.

Hiking time is an estimate, which depends on the speed *you* walk on varying terrain. In general, most people walk about three miles in one hour on level ground. Moderate uphill walking slows you down to about two miles per hour, and steep hills to one mile per hour or less. If you plan to walk slowly to enjoy the sights, or you stop frequently to examine or photograph flora or fauna, or take long lunch breaks, then expect to add to the stated hiking time.

Vertical rise refers to the total rise in elevation for the hike. If the hike is a steady uphill walk, vertical rise is the difference between the lowest and highest points on your route. In most cases, however, your hike will be an up-and-down affair; the vertical rise is the sum of all the hills you climb during your hike, and may be considerably more than the difference between the lowest and highest points on the terrain.

Map(s) may be one or more United States Geological Survey (USGS) topographic maps. All the USGS maps are in the 7½′ series, with the one exception of Gleasmans Falls, where one of the maps is 15′. Where other maps are available (such as park maps), note of these is made in the map summary.

Land Classification. The state uses different classifications for its land in and outside the Forest Preserve (which is part of the larger land area called the Adirondack Park). Within the Forest Preserve, state land has been divided into four categories: intensive use areas, primitive areas, wild forest areas, and wilderness areas. Other than footpaths, there is little that is manmade to be found in wilderness areas; wild forest areas, on the other hand, may include manmade objects such as roads, firetowers, radio antennas, and the like.

In the rest of New York, state lands fall into one of four categories: state forests, wildlife management areas, marsh units, and unique areas. While all state lands are administered for multi-use, there is considerable variation in primary use from one class of land to another.

State forests, for example, are managed mainly for lumbering and logging, which create revenue for the state. Wildlife management areas are maintained to support a sizable population of wildlife, such as deer, wild turkey, grouse, and various kinds of game birds. Marsh units in the upstate area are found mostly along the shores of Lake Ontario. The state established them to protect and preserve wetlands—the areas used by ducks, geese, and shore birds as resting, feeding, and nesting places.

Finally, the newest classification—unique area—covers land with physical, biological, and/or ecological properties that are unusual, fragile, or endangered and that need special supervision to be preserved and protected.

Hikes in this book will take you to most of these types of state land.

Some Helpful Information. Any well-stocked bookstore will provide you with dozens of books about hiking, camping, cross-country skiing, and snowshoeing. In addition, a number of public and private organizations in New York can give you specific information about public lands, hiking trails, and places to see. Finally, there are books and guides that can provide more detailed information about the history of a local region and about hiking areas within these regions.

Organizations and Clubs

Adirondack Mountain Club (ADK)
RD 3, Box 3055, Luzerne Rd.
Lake George, NY 12845
(518) 793-7737
Publishes regional guides and other publications for hikers. Many chapters throughout New York state conduct group outings and day hikes. Membership is currently $30 a year.

Finger Lakes Association
309 Lake Street
Penn Yan, NY 14527
(315) 536-7488
Issues an annual booklet, "Finger Lakes Regional Travel Guide," with information about motels and places to see.

Finger Lakes State Park and Recreation Commission.
Taughannock Falls State Park

R.D. 3, Park Road
Trumansburg, NY 14886
(607) 387-7041
Provides information on and maps of
state parks in the Finger Lakes region.

Finger Lakes Trail Conference, Inc.
P.O. Box 18048
Rochester, NY 14618
(716) 288-7191
Provides a guide to the map series
covering the Finger Lakes Trail system,
and information about the conference
and member hiking clubs. Current
membership is $10 a year.

State or County Offices

Department of Parks and Recreation
Onondaga County
Onondaga Lake Parkway
Liverpool, NY 13088
(318) 451-7275
Provides brochures, pamphlets, and
other literature on the county's forests,
parks and nature center as well as current listings of seasonal activities.

*New York State Department of
Environmental Conservation*
50 Wolf Road
Albany, NY 12233
(518) 474-2121
Provides brochures of state lands and
pamphlets on outdoor subjects, and publishes a magazine, *The Conservationist.*

New York State Division of Tourism
Department of Commerce
1 Commerce Plaza
Albany, NY 12245
(800) 225-5697 (within US) or
(518) 474-4116
Issues a State highway map, brochures
and pamphlets on various regions and
annual state travel guide.

*New York State Office of Parks, Recrea-
tion and Historic Preservation*
Empire State Plaza

Albany, NY 12238
(518) 474-0456
Issues an annual *Guide to New York
State Parks, Recreation & Historic Preservation* containing information about locations, telephone numbers, and facilities at
each site. The Office also issues a free
"Trails Across New York" map.

Books and Guides

Ehling, William P. *Canoeing Central New
York,* Woodstock, VT, Backcountry Publi-
cations, 1982.
——— *25 Ski Tours in Central New York,*
2nd ed., Woodstock, VT, Backcountry
Publications, 1987.
*Guide to Trails of the Finger Lakes
Region,* 6th ed., Ithaca, NY, Cayuga
Trails Club, 1987. Available from Finger
Lakes Trail Conference (see above).
Graham, Frank, Jr. *The Adirondack Park:
A Political History,* New York, Alfred A.
Knopf, 1978.
Jamieson, Paul F. and Donald Morris
Adirondack Canoe Waters: North Flow,
3rd ed., Glens Falls, NY, Adirondack
Mountain Club, 1988.
Jamieson, Paul F., *Adirondack Reader,*
New York, The Macmillan Co., 1964.
McMartin, Barbara, *Discover The South-
western Adirondacks,* Woodstock, VT,
Backcountry Publications, 1987.
——— *Fifty Hikes in the Adirondacks,*
2nd ed., Woodstock, VT, Backcountry
Publications, 1989.
Samson, Harold E. *Tug Hill Country:
Tales from the Big Woods,* Lakemont,
NY, North Country Books, 1971.
VanDiver, Bradford B. *Field Guide to
Upstate New York,* Dubuque, Kendall/
Hunt Publishing Co., 1980.
——— *Rocks and Routes of the North
Country New York,* Geneva, NY, W.F.
Humphrey Press, Inc., 1976.
Von Engeln, O.D. *The Finger Lakes
Region: Its Origin and Nature,* Ithaca,
Cornell University Press, 1961.

Finger Lakes Hills

1

Gannett Hill

Total distance: 11 miles
Hiking time: 5 hours
Vertical rise: 1,176 feet
Map: USGS 7½' Bristol Springs

This hike takes you through the magnificent mountainous country just west of the southern tip of Canandaigua Lake—an area variously known as the Bristol Hill region, the Gannett Hill section, and New York's Italian Alps.

"Mountainous" may be a bit of an overstatement. These "mountains" are no match for the European Alps, the western Rockies, or even the high peaks of the Adirondacks. Carved by glacial activity during the Pleistocene period, they are technically only hills, as they barely top out at 2,200 feet. But when you hike in this region, your senses insist that you are surrounded by mountains. From a distance, rugged, straight-sided, tree-covered forms dominate narrow valleys. And when you are on top of one of these hills, the world drops away at your feet with breathtaking suddenness, revealing spectacular views of the gorge-like valleys below.

Although the hills hereabouts do have an alpine appearance, you might well wonder why they are called "Italian." First, there are the local place names—Naples, Naples Creek, Italy Hill, and Italy Valley. Second, this is fine wine country. Vineyards grace the valleys and lower hill

Looking north up U-shaped valley from Gannett Hill

sections surrounding the village of Naples, the site of a major winery and hub of the local wine industry.

The hike starts in Ontario County Park on the top of Gannett Hill, the highest point in this region. Here you are at the northern end of a spur trail of the Finger Lakes Trail (FLT) system, the Bristol Hill Branch Trail. This trail, which is blazed orange, runs south 27 miles to intersect the main east-west Finger Lakes Trail about two miles northeast of Prattsburg. The hike described here, however, only uses part of the Bristol Hill Branch Trail, following it along the Gannett Hill ridge and then over Cleveland Hill to a dirt road. There you leave the trail and return to your start in the county park by way of dirt roads that run over Powell Hill and along the eastern edge of Gannett Hill. Because you do some hill climbing, this hike is best classified as moderate to difficult.

Access. You can reach Ontario County Park by following NY 21 north out of Naples for six miles to Bristol Springs. In this hamlet turn left onto NY 64 and continue 0.5 mile north to Gannett Hill Road. Turn left, and drive 1.5 miles to the park. There is a modest entry fee for your vehicle; a brochure and map of the park are

also available at the entrance (or you can obtain them in advance by writing: Division of Human Services, Ontario County, Canandaigua, NY 14424).

Leave your vehicle in the area near the sign pointing to the Jumpoff, and walk the short distance to this overlook. The Jumpoff is aptly named; once you reach the overlook there is nothing but daylight between you and the valley floor 800 feet below.

Trail. Beginning at the Jumpoff, your route follows the FLT spur trail to the left along the edge of the hill for about 100 yards, giving you an excellent view of the valley below, West Hollow to the south, and Berby Hollow to the north. It then swings left, taking you into the woods and onto the flatter land of the Gannett Hill ridge. It soon drops into a gully and then moves uphill for a little more than ¼ mile before again leveling out. At this point you are just to the right of Gannett Hill's summit, which at 2,256 feet is the highest point in the Bristol Hill region.

After another ¼ mile of relatively level walking, you begin a ½-mile descent into West Hollow. At the base of the hill, on level ground again, you pass an area used for tenting by hikers and soon break out of the woods into an open field. The trail now swings right (west) and in ¼ mile emerges on West Hollow Road (paved).

Cross the highway, turn right, and walk a short distance down the road until you pick up the Cleveland Hill section of the trail on your left, designated by a sign and orange trail markers. Once in the woods, you start uphill; the climb is steep and demanding, requiring you to make a 400-foot ascent in less than ½ mile. As you near the summit of Cleveland Hill, the land flattens considerably, and for almost a mile you walk the relatively level north-south ridge, passing over the crest (el. 2,200 feet) at midpoint.

When the trail eventually begins to descend Cleveland Hill's south side, it does so gradually. Over the next ½ mile, however, the slope becomes more pronounced, and the final pitch before the base is quite sharp. When you reach the bottom the trail leads you across an open field (used by Scouts as a camping area) to a jeep trail that brings you to a dirt road.

Here you leave the Bristol Hill Branch Trail. Turn left (east) and walk the short distance to West Hollow Road. Turn left again and continue north on this road for ½ mile until you come to Porter Road. Turn right onto this dirt road, which runs east through the flatland of West Hollow. Because of the open fields on both sides of the road, you have an excellent view of High Point Hill and Cleveland Hill to the west and Powell Hill to the north.

In 1½ miles you reach Powell Hill Road. Again you turn left and walk north. The first mile is over level ground. Then the road begins to rise as it bends westward, coming gradually up the east side of Powell Hill. Another ½-mile walk brings you to the summit (el. 2,000 feet). To the east you have a grand view of the Naples Creek Valley and Canandaigua Lake beyond. The road now levels out, making the three-mile walk back to Ontario County Park and your vehicle relatively easy.

The park also boasts numerous well-marked trails that tie into the southbound Finger Lakes branch trail. It makes a good base for a weekend outing, and several campsites are available for overnight camping.

In winter, snowshoeing along the Bristol Hill trail can be fun. Once the snow comes, it packs well and stays a long time. Although sections in the flatlands and valleys are ideal for cross-country skiing, generally this is not the place for ski touring; the hill trails are a bit too steep to negotiate with Nordic skis.

Taughannock Falls State Park

Total distance: 4¼ miles
Hiking time: 2½ hours
Vertical rise: 559 feet
Map: USGS 7½' Ludlowville

This short 4¼-mile hike takes you around and into an impressively deep gorge to the west of Cayuga Lake where the most striking attraction is Taughannock Falls. Plunging 215 feet into a 30-foot-deep pool, this falls is 55 feet higher than Niagara Falls. In fact, it is one of the highest falls in the eastern United States. In the spring when the waters from melting snow rush into the upper end of the gorge and plunge over the crest, the falls becomes an awesome and breathtaking spectacle. Standing at the base, dwarfed by 400-foot walls that form an immense amphitheater, you will find yourself swept up in the beauty and grandeur.

There are several versions of the origin of the name "Taughannock" (pronounced Tau-han-nok). According to one account, the name originated with the Indian word "Taghkanic," meaning "the great fall in the woods." A more interesting legend ties the name to a Taughannock chieftain of the Delaware tribes, who controlled the lands southeast of the Finger Lakes Region into Pennsylvania. The chieftain, who had been forced to relinquish claim to certain lands, led a band of warriors on a mission of revenge against the Cayugas. The mission was ill-fated, the chieftain fell in battle, and his body was

hurled into the gorge near the falls, which have born the name Taughannock ever since.

Although it is a bit less dramatic, the geological origin of the falls makes an interesting story, too. The rock layer that forms the base of the gorge and the streambed of Taughannock Creek is Tully limestone, a hard, enduring mineral. The walls of the lower gorge are all black Geneseo shale, which has a crumbly composition. During the post-glacial period, the water quickly eroded this rock, washing it downstream to Lake Cayuga to form a large delta that is now the site of the North Point and South Point sections of the state park. Water erosion of the Geneseo shale halted in the lower gorge when the Tully limestone was reached and in the middle of the gorge when Sherburne sandstone was exposed. The sections of harder rock that were not eroded eventually stood high above the lower streambed, and Taughannock Falls was born.

There are three trails in the 825-acre Taughannock Falls State Park. The trails that run along both rims of the gorge are known as the North Rim Trail and the South Rim Trail. A third trail, the Gorge Trail, runs from the parking lot at the lower end of the gorge to the foot of Taughannock Falls. There, on the north side of Taughannock Creek, a specially-constructed observation area permits you to view the falls head-on.

Access. To reach your starting point at the upper end of the gorge, take NY 96 north from Ithaca or south from Waterloo to the village of Jacksonville. In the center of the village, turn north onto Jacksonville Road, and drive 1.8 miles to the bridge over Taughannock Creek. Park your vehicle in the area on the south side of the bridge.

Trail. Walk across the bridge, and pick up the foot-trail on your right. It runs up a small embankment and into a clump of trees. A few feet into the trees you will see a footbridge. (Just before you cross the bridge, you encounter a sign reading "Trail" on the left. It points to a self-guided nature trail that runs along the south side of Taughannock Creek. You can obtain a printed guide to it from the park office at the lower end of the gorge.)

Walk to the middle of the footbridge. To your right (southwest), the water of Taughannock Creek plummets 100 feet down a sloping caprock into a plunge pool. This marks the beginning of the upper gorge system. To your left (northeast), the gorge becomes deeper, with walls that rise 200 feet straight up.

Retrace your steps to the trail and follow it to the right (northeast) alongside Falls Road (paved) for ½ mile to a parking area. To your right, two observation points have been constructed to give you excellent head-on views of Taughannock Falls. The topmost vantage point is level with the parking area; the other is lower and somewhat closer to the falls.

You can now start your hike on the North Rim Trail, which begins at the east end of this parking area and affords you some fine views directly into the gorge. The trail pitches gradually downhill; near the end its slope is more pronounced,

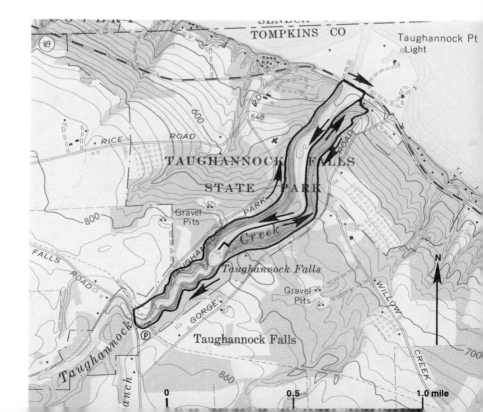

until it brings you out of the woods onto NY 89. Across the highway a picnic area on the delta of eroded Geneseo shale fronts on Cayuga Lake.

Turn right onto the highway and walk over the bridge that crosses Taughannock Creek. Look upstream to the wide rock formation that forms a small falls. Continue another 200 feet to a parking area for the lower gorge on your right. You are now ready to follow the ¾-mile-long Gorge Trail. Signs point the way. The gorge is quite wide here, and so is the tree-shaded trail. As you walk toward the falls, you pass through a stand of trees; the base of the gorge first narrows and then widens again. On your left you will notice the piles of crumbly Geneseo shale along the side of the gorge wall.

As you near the falls, the trail turns right and crosses a footbridge, taking you to an observation platform right near the falls and plunge pool.

After you have taken in the spectacular sight, retrace your steps to parking area on NY 89. Here you can easily find the South Rim Trail for the return route to your vehicle. At first, the trail ascends sharply through the woods to the gorge rim. From here on it is relatively flat. Like the North Rim Trail, it runs along the edge of the gorge, allowing you to look down 400 feet to the floor.

In ¼ mile from the trail's end on Jacksonville Road, you come to a spot where you can look directly down on the falls. The crest is 200 feet below and the plunge pool 251 feet below that. It is an unusual and exciting vantage point.

Sugar Hill State Forest

Total distance: 5 miles
Hiking time: 2½ hours
Vertical rise: 750 feet
Maps: USGS 7½' Reading Center; USGS 7½' Wayne

October is the best time to hike at Sugar Hill. The air is cool, the sky is clear, and the autumn foliage for which the area is famous is at its peak. In fact, to walk Sugar Hill in the fall is to walk through a color explosion, for you are awash in waves of yellow, red, crimson, gold, blue, and purple as the sunlight streams in from all sides through beech, oak, hickory, maple, and ash trees. It is an experience that will sharpen your senses and quicken your spirit.

The design of the trail system here is ideal to allow you to take in the richness of the season. You pass through hardwood stands, down tree-lined lanes, and across deserted farmlands that have now become the territory of saplings and young trees. A network of roads gives easy access to all the trails, and the choices open to the hiker are almost unlimited.

Sugar Hill State Forest covers 9,085 acres of hill country between the southern tip of Seneca Lake in the east and Waneta Lake and Lamoka Lake in the west. Atop the area's highest point on the northern edge of the state forest is the Sugar Hill Recreational Area, a state-operated site where you can picnic, camp, and climb a firetower for a spectacular view of the rugged hill country to the south. There is an archery range nearby, and trails for hikers and horseback riders radiate from the parking lot.

Access. The hike recommended here begins on County Route 21 about 0.6 mile south of Tower Hill Road, at the point where the Finger Lakes Trail (FLT) crosses. This puts you within easy reach of three lean-tos and offers you some fine overlooks facing east toward Seneca Lake.

To reach your starting point, take County Route 28 west out of Watkins Glen (located at the southern tip of Seneca Lake). About a mile out of town, County Route 28 runs into County Route 23; fork left onto County Route 23 and drive about six miles until you see a sign on the right directing you to turn left for the Sugar Hill Recreational Area.

This turn puts you on County Route 21. Drive south for a mile to cross Tower Hill Road. From Tower Hill Road, you continue for 0.6 mile to where an abandoned road crosses County Route 21. Park here, for the abandoned road is a section of the FLT (blazed white) on which you will begin your hike.

Trail. Start your hike by walking east on the abandoned road, identified on the USGS map as Sickler Road. Although it doubles as a horse trail, no motorized vehicles are allowed.

The road is tree-lined for part of the way, but soon it becomes more open as you pass through fields where saplings and small trees have just begun to take over. After about ¼ mile, a trail marker points to your left (north). Turn here and follow the FLT as it crosses another abandoned field, dips into a gully, and passes through a wooded area. The trail soon turns right (east) and crosses aspen stands, wooded areas, and more abandoned fields until it brings you to the first of the three lean-tos.

There is an old, unused wagon road behind the lean-to; it swings north and offers an alternative route by which you can return to County Route 21. Your hike, however, continues on the FLT, which passes in front of the lean-to, taking you southeast through some open areas and back into the forest on some high ground. Watch on your left for the deep cut formed by Glen Creek—the creek that eventually flows into the deep Watkins Glen Gorge, some three miles to the east. In this area the cut is known as Van Zandt Hollow.

The FLT follows the western edge of the hollow until it encounters a feeder stream. Here it turns right (west) for a short distance, crosses the stream at a low spot, and heads back in an easterly direction to Sickler Road.

At this point, the FLT turns left (east) toward Watkins Glen. Your route, however, follows Sickler Road to the right (west), heading uphill through a wooded area. You soon cross an open stretch and pass the point where you earlier turned off Sickler Road. A short walk brings you back to your vehicle.

You may stop now, but the recommended hike continues west on Sickler Road (which is also the FLT here) for about ¼ mile through a heavily wooded

Author taking a breather along the trail

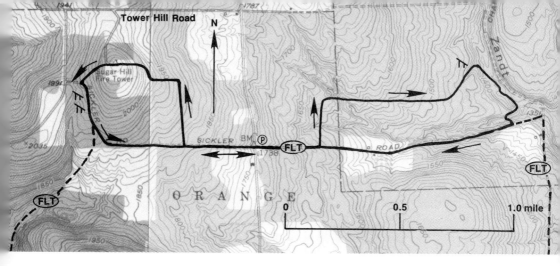

area. Remain on the FLT as it turns off to the right (north) to climb toward the recreational area at the top of Sugar Hill (el. 2,080 feet).

The firetower atop Sugar Hill offers you some striking views of the surrounding landscape. You may wish to stop here for lunch or a rest before you return to the FLT and continue your hike downhill past two more lean-tos and a horse barn.

You now find yourself back on Sickler Road. Bear left (south). After ¼ mile the road curves left (east), but the FLT continues straight on a southerly course. Re-main on Sickler Road and walk eastward for about a mile to return to County Route 21 and your vehicle.

This area is actively used during the winter months by snowmobilers and ski tourers. The hiking trail is particularly suited for ski touring, for it crosses varied terrain, adding zest and challenge to a fine day's skiing. The snow is plentiful here, and it packs well in the forest area and on the trails, providing excellent ski conditions during January, February, and March.

Hi Tor Wildlife Management Area

Total distance: 7 miles
Hiking time: 4 hours
Vertical rise: 1,010 feet
Maps: USGS 7½' Naples; USGS 7½' Prattsburg;
  USGS 7½' Middlesex

Hi Tor has a distinctive sound to it. "Tor" is an Old English word meaning high, craggy place or, perhaps more picturesquely, a high rock or pile of rocks on a hilltop. It probably comes from the Old Welsh "turr" or the Old Celtic "tur." (While the USGS topo maps refer to "High Tor," the state's Department of Environmental Conservation (DEC) uses "Hi Tor" on its signs, so this is the spelling we'll follow here.)

The land on which Hi Tor Wildlife Management Area is located pretty well matches its name. It is made up of highlands and marsh lands and includes deep, narrow valleys, cut by the glaciers that overrode New York more than 12,000 years ago, as well as hills and valleys on top of hills. These are steep hills, straight-shouldered and heavily-forested. They also are deeply cut and clefted by streams that give the area its gullies, gorges, and eroded cliffs.

Hence, a craggy hilltop is a good description of the area, much of which is quite scenic, and the hiker can see it all, even when walking through the woods along the edge of a gorge.

Hi Tor maintains its English connection by keeping close company with such places as South Bristol, Bristol Springs, Pulteney, and Middlesex, but in the best European tradition it also has the Latin neighbors of Naples, West Italy Hill, and Italy Valley.

Hi Tor Wildlife Management Area is made up of a number of closely-situated but separate units, two of which are quite large. The largest is a 3,920-acre parcel on the high hills immediately east of the village of Naples. Just north of this hilly section is a 1,000-acre marsh in the lowlands bordering the south end of Canandaigua Lake. A third parcel, still further north, is called South Hill, which, according to legend, was the birthplace of the Seneca Indians, one of the tribes of the Iroquois Confederacy. As they occupied land in the western Finger Lakes region, they were called "keepers of the western door" of the confederacy.

Hi Tor's major attraction for the hiker today is its trail system. Running through the large southern portion of Hi Tor is the Bristol Hill Branch of the Finger Lakes Trail (FLT). This 27-mile-long spur trail begins at Ontario Park on Gannett Hill (see Hike 1) and intersects the FLT trunk trail about two miles northeast of Prattsburg.

Looking across meadow at Hi Tor

Access. The trailhead to Hi Tor's hike-able trails can be reached from Naples. To reach Naples take NY 21 from Dansville or Wayland in the west or from Canandaigua or Manchester in the north (Manchester is at exit 43 of I-90). In Naples, drive to the southern end of the village on NY 21. Just south of the village is a fork, with NY 21 taking the right leg and NY 53 taking the left. Turn onto NY 53 and follow it south for 1.3 miles where a paved road (County Route 21) intersects on the left.

Turn here and drive uphill on County Route 21 (which becomes Italy Valley Road). After 2 miles you enter Hi Tor Wildlife Management Area and almost immediately reach Bassett Road on the left. Italy-Naples Church is on the far corner. Turn onto Bassett Road and drive north for 0.15 mile. The road now turns right (east), and another 0.15 mile brings you to a parking area on the left adjoining a dirt road running north. This is the trailhead and the continuation of the Bristol Hill Branch of the FLT leading into Hi Tor Park.

Trail. About half of your hiking in Hi Tor is on walking paths marked FLT, or blazed in orange (indicating it is part of the Bristol Hill spur trail which joints the main FLT trail further to the southeast;

the other half is on state truck trails, dirt roads which run north-south and east-west. In the past, the FLT entered Hi Tor about a mile downhill on East Hill Road; but in 1984, it was re-routed to enter from Bassett Road.

The terrain around the trailhead is flat, allowing an easy hiking start. Your hike takes you north on the truck trail which begins next to the parking area; 500 feet brings you to a barrier restricting vehicular traffic. Circle around the barrier and continue north for 0.2 mile where the road forks. The right leg is the one you will use when you return. For now, however, your route is the left fork. This truck trail runs west a short distance over a small stream where it turns north into a thick stand of trees marking the beginning of the Hi Tor forest. Over the stream, the terrain changes, rising sharply on your left. At the stream, the elevation is 1,460 feet; at the top of Hi Tor the vertical distance of your climb will be 400 feet. This climb on the truck trail is done in just one mile in a relatively straight line cutting through the Hi Tor forest.

Near the top, you intersect another truck trail running east-west. The trail on which you are walking continues across the east-west truck trail, and you can see orange markers on the trees

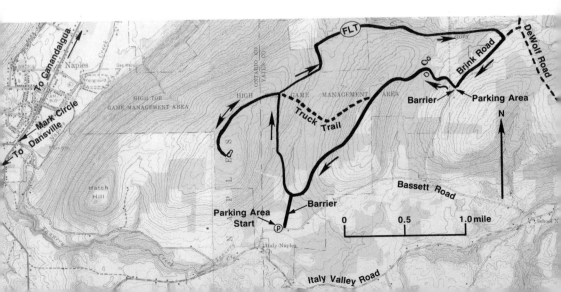

ahead. The intersection, however, is the place to turn for a side-trip to a man-made pond. So turn left on the east-west truck trail; initially this route runs west, but it soon begins to turn south, eventually to form a quarter circle.

The terrain here is relatively level, rising slightly until the truck trail almost touches the Hi Tor boundary on your right, about 1/2 mile from the intersection of the two truck trails where your side-trip began. A few steps westward on the former FLT trail bring you to the edge of open but private land with a westward view; the land pitches downward toward Naples in the valley at the foot of the small but peaked Hatch Hill.

Return to the truck trail and continue walking for another 0.2 mile where you find a pond in a most unlikely place—a broad level area in the wood which, nonetheless, constitutes one of Hi Tor's high spots with an elevation of 1,880 feet. There is, however, enough of a pitch to form a shallow basin, just enough of a depression to collect water being slowly released by the surrounding forest. This is a water hole for deer and forest animals as well as a resting and feeding pond for waterfowl.

Retrace your steps back to the intersection and turn left onto the truck trail with FLT markers. Follow this truck trail as it swings to the northeast and heads downhill. At the 1/2-mile mark, the marked trail turns left off the dirt road into the forest to take you to an overlook with a fine view to the north of Canandaigua Lake and South Hill.

The trail swings right and soon crosses the road on which you walked earlier; a little over 1/4 mile more and a gradual descent brings you to the edge of an impressively deep gorge (Conklin Gully). The trail stays on the south rim of the gorge as it heads east.

This Conklin Gully trail section is a delight. It is scenic, relatively flat, and cool even on hot days. The gorge becomes less deep and a little wider, until after one mile it is quite shallow. The trail now climbs a small hill and swings south away from the gully. In 1/2 mile more, you come to a dirt road, Brink Road.

If you want to add two more miles to your hike, you can follow the FLT left on Brink Road to DeWolf Road, where either a right or left turn will bring you to overlooks. The more scenic choice is the southern route of the FLT that reaches the top of West Italy Hill with a view across Italy Valley.

Back at the spot where the trail intersected Brink Road, a turn right onto Brink Road takes you in little over 1/2 mile to a parking area on the north side of the road. Running west from Brink Road is a single-lane truck trail. A barrier at the start prevents unauthorized vehicles from using it, but you can turn right here and follow the dirt road downhill.

In less than 1/2 mile, you come to an open area and a series of ponds, one on the south side of the road and two on the north side. The trail soon leaves the field-like area, enters the woods, and heads gradually uphill. About 1/2 mile brings you to a fork; take the left leg, and continue in a southwesterly direction.

A short distance south from the intersection on your left you pass a knob, 60 feet above the road; this hilltop is Hi Tor's highest spot (el. 1,900 feet). It is not, however, the area's highest elevation; that's found further east about 1½ mile away on what is called West Italy Hill (el. 2,040 feet), over which the FLT passes in its eastward journey.

Once past Hi Tor's high spot, the truck trail starts its descent through the forest, dropping 400 feet in a mile. As the road nears the bottom, it turns to the right; about 0.1 mile brings you to a fork, the one you encountered when you started your hike. At the fork, turn left (south); 0.2 mile brings you to the road barrier and to your vehicle.

5

Enfield Glen/Treman State Park

Total distance: 9½ miles
Hiking time: 5 hours
Vertical rise: 1,020 feet
Maps: USGS 7½′ Mecklenburg; USGS 7½′ Ithaca
West

Call it the Enfield Connection, a section of the Finger Lakes Trail (FLT) that connects two large pieces of state land: Connecticut Hill State Wildlife Management Area in the west and Robert H. Treman State Park in the east. In between are high spots that give you fine, wide views of distant ridges—some of them 20 and 30 miles away. You'll walk in quiet glens and cool forests, along abandoned wagon roads meandering through stands of maples, beeches, and oaks, and over sparkling brooks. Finally, you'll enter a deep gorge cut by Enfield Creek and arrive at Lucifer Falls, an impressive piece of natural sculpturing where a waterfall tumbles 150 feet down a slanted rock face between towering gorge walls.

The Enfield Glen is a post-glacial, water-eroded gorge running through the heart of Treman Park. While this is not one of the larger gorges of the Finger Lakes Region, it is a spectacular sight, with walls 300 feet high, falls, narrow passages, and chutes. A paved trail system allows you to walk through the gorge itself.

The section of the FLT described here has no official name, but Enfield Trail seems appropriate, as the village of Enfield is a short distance northeast of the

starting point, and the trail crosses Enfield Creek at the upper end of Enfield Glen in Treman Park.

Access. The best approach to the trailhead follows NY 13 south out of Ithaca for three miles to the intersection with NY 327, which forks to the right. Turn onto NY 327 and drive west 4.9 miles to the intersection with Harvey Hill Road at Bostwick Corners.

Turn left (west) onto Harvey Hill Road and travel two miles to the first intersection; turn left (south) on Black Oak Road and drive one mile to Connecticut Hill Road. Turn left (east) and drive another

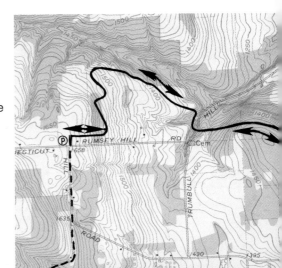

0.8 mile, where Connecticut Hill Road turns right (south) and Rumsey Hill Road continues straight ahead (east). Park your car at the corner, where you will see the white blazes of the FLT.

Trail. Follow the blazes east, downhill along Rumsey Hill Road for about 200 yards where the FLT turns onto a farm road on your left. The road runs past a barn (which sits about 25 yards off the road), across a field, and onto an abandoned wagon trail canopied by trees. At the barn and along this part of the FLT you have a fine view of distant hills to your right (east); the first ridge is Jersey Hill in the Danby Region just south of Ithaca.

About ½ mile from Rumsey Hill Road, the FLT enters a wooded area and then starts a moderate descent into a gully. At the base of the slope is a small unnamed brook, which flows east for two miles to empty into Enfield Creek. The FLT crosses the brook, then turns sharply right and follows it southeast for about ¾ mile on another abandoned wagon road, crossing a small feeder stream en route. This is a most pleasant walk through a wooded glen. The trail here is wide, and in summer the brook murmurs gently as it flows through the cool, green glen.

Soon you emerge from the glen onto

Trumbull Hill Road (paved). Turn left here and follow the white trail markers down the road for about 100 yards. Here the trail turns left into a wooded area, and a few more steps bring you to the brook you were following earlier.

The trail crosses the brook and heads uphill for about 150 yards, where it turns onto still another abandoned wagon road. The trail is relatively flat, following the contour of a hill that rises on your right, and it takes you through a wooded area and a pleasant evergreen stand. Through the woods to your left are fields, and from time to time you encounter clearings that allow you to look northeast over rolling farmland to another range of hills.

From Trumbull Hill Road it is only ½ mile to Porter Hill Road. Here again you will be treated to a fine view of the countryside to the north and east.

Cross Porter Hill Road, and follow the markers into a small wooded area, then continue on a straight easterly course. You pass alternately through open areas and small wooded sections until you reach Hines Road one mile east of Porter Hill Road. The trail crosses Hines Road and follows a hedgerow bordering fields to your left and right before reaching the edge of a wooded area. It then edges the woods, gradually swinging southeast

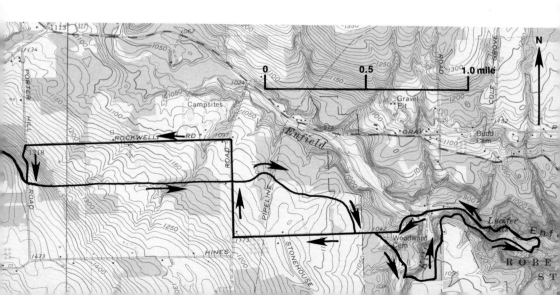

until it reaches Woodward Road (dirt).

Turn left on Woodward Road. After a short distance, the trail forks right onto another, unmarked dirt road. The white trail blazes take you down this road 500 yards to a bridge crossing Fish Kill, a clean, attractive stream that flows into Enfield Creek at the upper end of Treman Park. Follow the FLT across the bridge to a dirt road about 100 feet beyond. Turn left on this road and walk to the top of a hill where the trail enters the woods on your left to follow a high rim overlooking Fish Kill. There is a clear view here to the northwest.

Follow the trail through the evergreens and hardwoods until you emerge on yet another abandoned road. As you step on the road you are leaving Treman Park. Turn left and within a short distance a sign on your left tells you that you have again re-entered Treman State Park.

The FLT follows this road as it bends sharply to the right and heads southeast. About 250 yards from the bend, the FLT forks right and heads uphill. It is at this junction that you stop following the FLT. Instead, continue straight ahead on the abandoned road another 200 yards as it runs eastward through a pleasant hardwood area, where the trees canopy the road, to an intersection with a paved footpath.

This is one of the park's hiking trails, built and maintained by the state. Turn right and in a short distance you come to your first overlook, with a view east into the gorge.

Continue a short distance to the second overlook. Here you can view Lucifer Falls head-on from the south rim. The drop to the circular plunge pool at the base of the falls is about 300 feet. During the spring when the creek waters are high, the sight is impressive. A short walk beyond this overlook brings you to stone stairs, which take you down into the gorge to a footbridge across Enfield Creek. On the other side is the Gorge Trail. Turn left here and follow this trail along the edge of the gorge back to Lucifer Falls for still another, but closer, view of the falls.

The footpath then takes you past several smaller falls, back over the creek and into the Upper Picnic Area, a pleasant spot to rest and have lunch. Follow the road out of the park a short distance to Woodward Road; 150 yards along that road brings you to the point where you turned off earlier to reach Fish Kill.

You now can return to your vehicle via Woodward Road, turning right onto Hines Road and then left on Rockwell Road to the FLT, which takes you to Trumbull Hill Road. Turn left on Trumbull Hill Road and then right onto Rumsey Hill Road to your vehicle.

In winter, most of the route can be snowshoed and even skied, with the exception of the Gorge Trail. The land is high, and snowfall is good during January and February. Keep in mind that there are brooks to cross and some moderate climbing.

Connecticut Hill Wildlife Management Area

Total distance: 15 miles (two days)
Hiking time: 7 hours
Vertical rise: 2,010 feet
Maps: USGS 7½′ Alpine; USGS 7½′ Mecklenburg

As a landform, Connecticut Hill resembles a fat finger pointing south. On the east and west sides as well as at the finger tip, the forested land drops off precipitously, sometimes over 700 feet to the narrow valley floor that partly encircles the southern half of the hill.

Across the top of the hill is a large tract of state land known officially as the Connecticut Hill Wildlife Management Area. Five miles wide and seven miles long, it sits astride two counties, Schuyler County on the west and Tompkins County on the east. At 11,654 acres, the wildlife management area is the largest in New York.

Topographically, the hill is composed of a series of ridges, knobby or peaked hills, and valleys, many deeply dissected by small streams to form impressive gullies and gorges. The southern half of the hill, clefted and cut in all directions, is best described as craggy and rugged. The central section is a bit more level, but the landscape is still rolling. It is the nearest thing to an alpine area that this region has, which is what must have inspired the founders of the two hamlets at the southern tip of the hill—Alpine and Alpine Junction (site of the old Lehigh Valley railroad station). Local people just call the area the "Hill."

Why the name "Connecticut" in the middle of New York State? The reason is that the state of Connecticut acquired the land in 1800 and held it for 50 years before selling to private owners. One of the later owners was R. H. Treman, after whom Treman State Park, located a short distance southwest of Ithaca, is named.

The height of the hill is much the same as that of other hills in the landform region called the Finger Lakes Hills, which is at the northern edge of the Appalachian Plateau. The highest spot (el. 2,099 feet) is a knob with a radio tower and several antenna dishes at the northern edge of the state forest. Other high spots are Rowell Hill (el. 1,840 feet) in the east, VanLone Hill (el. 1,730 feet) in the west, and Swan Hill (el. 1,700 feet) in the southwest. In between, there are over a dozen unnamed hilltops that range from 1,830 to 2,010 feet.

Ecologically, the hill is unique, with probably as diversified a mixture of trees, shrubs, and plants as can be found in this part of New York. It is rich in evergreens (pines, hemlocks, and cedars) and hardwoods (ranging from cockspur hawthorne to sugar maple).

The hill was settled by the late 1700s, and by the mid-nineteenth century much of it had been cleared for cultivation and pasture. The number of farms had peaked by 1880 when, as in the case of many hilltop farms across the state's southern tier, farmers found that the poorly drained, low fertility clay soil could no longer support competitive agriculture. By 1926, only 20 of the original 109 farms were still operating; the rest stood idle or abandoned. During the Great Depression, New York acquired the farmland through the Federal Resettlement Administration, which helped farmers relocate by purchasing their land.

In the 1950s, the state initiated serious silvicultural practices to improve both timber quality and deer browse. For the professional conservationists, the state land became a giant outdoor laboratory in methods to arrest woodland succession. Potholes were blasted for waterfowl, and mowing and burning kept fields open, while clearcutting and selective cutting were used to create openings in mature forest. Maintenance of habitat diversity has become the identifying mark of the wildlife area.

As a result, the land supports a sizable deer herd, large numbers of ruffed grouse, and large flocks of wild turkey, among other sorts of wildlife that probably you will see while on your hike. Connecticut Hill is also a great place for birding; you'll spot dozens of species ranging from the Eastern wood pewee and brown thrasher to the vireos and warblers. Woodland flowers range from pink azaleas to the pointed blue-eyed grasses and pink ladyslippers.

To get a feel for this unusual land and to enjoy its many picturesque vistas, you have to spend several days on the hill, or at least camp for a weekend. Camping is allowed only by permit, which you can obtain by writing or calling the Regional Wildlife Manager, P.O. Box 1169, Cortland, NY 13045 (607-753-3095).

Access. The top of the hill can be reached from all sides. The commonly used routes, however, are Black Oak Road in the north, Connecticut Hill Road and Carter Creek Road in the southeast, and Swan Hill Road (which runs out of Alpine) in the southwest. We suggest

Old tree root system next to trail

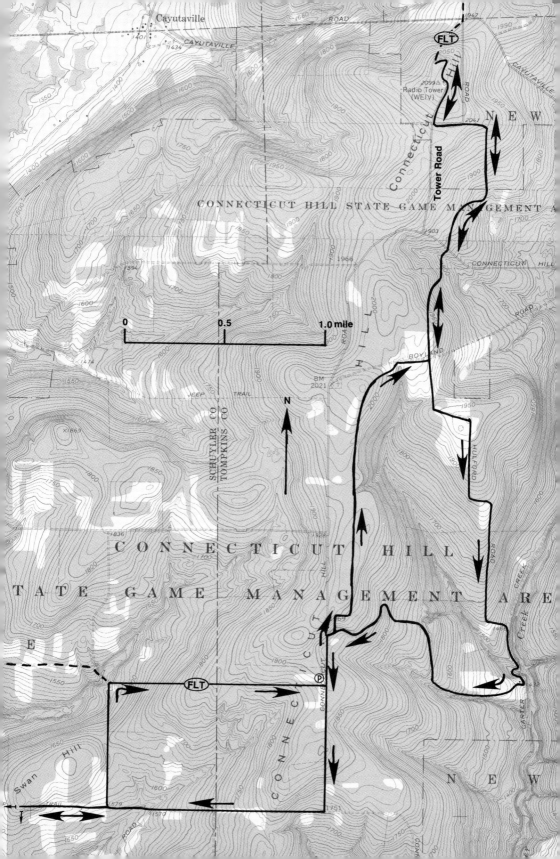

using the Connecticut Hill Road, which can be reached via NY 13 – 14 miles south of Ithaca in Pony Hollow, or 14.6 miles north of Horseheads. Turn west onto the Connecticut Hill Road (a dirt road), and drive uphill 2.6 miles where you will see two white blazes on a tree, marking the spot where the Finger Lakes Trail intersects the road. Park here.

Trail. The 15-mile trail system suggested here is for those who plan to camp overnight. If you wish, you can pitch your tent in the open area next to the road where you parked your car, or you can backpack to some other spot along the trail. Spots that are ideal for tenting include the open area at the corner of Boyland and Hulford Roads, a half mile south on Hulford Road, and off the road south of Swan Hill. But there are many other places you may find to your liking in the woods themselves.

First Day

Connecticut Hill Road and back via Finger Lakes Trail and Hulford Road
Distance: 8.8 miles
Hiking time: 4½ hours

For the first day's loop, follow the white blazes of the Finger Lakes Trail (FLT) from your parking spot north along Connecticut Hill Road for ¼ mile, where the FLT turns right off the road and enters a stand of large red pine. A short distance into the forest, the trail turns left and heads straight north for just a little over a mile, where it begins to turn to the right. A short distance further brings you to Boyland Road; follow this road for less than ¼ mile where the trail turns left onto a lane. A little way down the lane, the FLT leaves the lane and turns right as it heads downhill into the forest.

This downhill stretch takes you in a little over ½ mile to Connecticut Hill Road. The trail exits onto the road, follows it for

about 100 yards, and then turns left up an embankment into the forest. The trail dips down a bit at first but then starts to slope upward for a little over ½ mile where it makes a 90-degree turn to the left onto an abandoned farm road. A ¼ mile more brings you to the corner of Black Oak Road; continue west a short distance on this dirt road to where you see Tower Road intersecting on the right. Follow Tower Road north past the radio tower and antenna dishes for almost ½ mile to a picnic area with several tables and fireplaces.

This part of the state land is managed by the Park Commission rather than by the Department of Environmental Conservation (DEC). No camping is permitted here, but with its picnic tables it is an ideal spot for a lunch break or a rest. If you follow the FLT blazes from the picnic area a short distance to Cayutaville Road, you'll come to an open area with a fine view of the hill country in the west.

Retrace your steps southward for 2.5 miles to the Boyland-Hulford Road intersection. Turn onto Hulford Road, and follow it southward for a little less than ½ mile. On both sides of the road are fields maintained by the DEC. You are also at one of the area's high spots, which gives you a nice overlook to the south toward the hilltops of Newfield State Forest four miles away.

The walk for the next mile is all downhill through the forest with a couple of fields en route. As you near the bottom, the road turns left and then follows the west edge of a deep ravine through which flows Carter Creek. A ¼ mile further, the road crosses a bridge over a small brook and then heads uphill and westward through a fairly large open area. Soon you are back in the forest with the trees shading the road as you climb upward for a little over a mile, eventually reaching Connecticut Hill Road. Turn left (south) here; a short distance brings you back to your vehicle and to your tent if you're camping here.

Second Day

Connecticut Hill Road and back via Swan Hill and Finger Lakes Trail
Distance: 3.6 miles
Hiking time: 2 hours

For the second loop, follow Connecticut Hill Road from your vehicle south for a little over ½ mile; here the road turns left, while another unnamed dirt road turns right. Turn right (west) on that road. It pitches downward for just over ½ mile, passes Swan Hill Road forking off on the left, crosses a small brook, and then starts to rise.

About ¼ mile from Swan Hill Road, the dirt road turns 90 degrees and heads north. Continuing due west, or straight ahead, however, is a lane. If you stay on this lane for ¼ mile, you will find excellent views to the west and to the south from an open area on Swan Hill.

Retrace your steps to the intersection. Turn left (north) here, and follow the road due north for about ½ mile. About the halfway point, you get another view, this time to the north; from here the road slopes downward until it reaches a narrow valley with a small brook. Just before you reach the bridge crossing this brook, you will spot the white blazes of the FLT, which enters the forest on your right.

Turn right onto the FLT, and follow it due east. It will take you uphill most of the way, leveling out as you near the trail's intersection with Connecticut Hill Road and the spot where you parked your vehicle.

7

Fillmore Glen State Park/Summer Hill State Forest

Total distance: 8 miles
Hiking time: 4½ hours
Vertical rise: 830 feet
Maps: USGS 7½′ Sempronius; USGS 7½′ Moravia

It may have been a place like Summer Hill State Forest that moved the poet Winston O. Abbott to write the invitation: "Come climb my hill and share with me/The quietude of woodland paths/ . . . Evening skies splashed with crimson fires of sunset/ . . . Come share these things of beauty." Indeed, the things of beauty are many here, and the hill is not difficult to climb. Combine Summer Hill with its neighbor, Fillmore Glen State Park—a deep, tree-greened cleft in Summer Hill's western slope—and you have a piece of earth where you can feel what one naturalist called "the land's heartbeat."

The name of the state forest is a good clue to its delights, for the ideal time to hike its trails is during the early summer when the fields and trees have turned a deep green, the air is warm, and the sky is a clean, clear blue. It is then that Summer Hill, like the flowering dogwood blossoms you encounter along your way, is at its best.

Although the state forest land has a checkerboard appearance on the map, it is large (4,345 acres) and completely forested, primarily with evergreens. It sits atop a set of gentle hills that form a plateau with an average elevation of 1,600 feet. To the west the land pitches sharply

down to the towns of Locke and Moravia, which sit in a narrow, glacial valley, while to the east it slopes more gently down to the hamlet of Dresserville.

The eight-mile loop recommended here allows you to take in the sights and sounds of both Summer Hill State Forest and Fillmore Glen State Park. It starts in the cool green of Summer Hill's woodlands and then takes you down along the southern rim of Fillmore Glen to its western end, back up the ravine trail past a small but beautiful lake, along the top of Summer Hill with its expansive western vista, and back through stately evergreens to your starting point.

On this hike you also can mix a little history with your walking. The name Fillmore honors Millard Fillmore, the man who became America's thirteenth president after Zachary Taylor died in office in 1850. Fillmore was a New Yorker, and the state has not forgotten its native son. The site of his birthplace, just outside state forest lands, can be reached by Fillmore Road, and a replica of the cabin where he was born is found at the entrance to Fillmore Glen State Park.

Here you can also see evidence of events that occurred much much earlier. During the Pleistocene epoch, continental glaciers invaded New York state, leaving their imprint in the Finger Lakes area with a variety of landforms. These include the rounded, worn-down hilltops, flattened uplands, deeply grooved valleys, and the small, rounded, and sometimes elongated hills called eskers or kames, formed by gravel and sand deposits from glacial streams or from debris that fell into openings in the retreating or stagnant ice.

Water erosion in the post-glacial period shaped many rock gorges and ravines found throughout the Finger Lakes Region. One such gorge is in Fillmore Glen State Park; into it a tributary stream plunges 800 feet from the top of the Summer Hill tableland down the steeply pitched slopes to Owasco Lake. During the post-glacial period, waters ate through the underlying shale and sandstone to form a winding chasm with spectacular cascades, chutes, and falls. As you walk, evidence of glaciation and post-glacial erosion is all around you, giving the area its unique mixture of gentle and rugged landscape.

Access. Summer Hill can be reached easily from Moravia, about five miles south of Owasco Lake. In Moravia, take NY 38 south to NY 90 in the village of

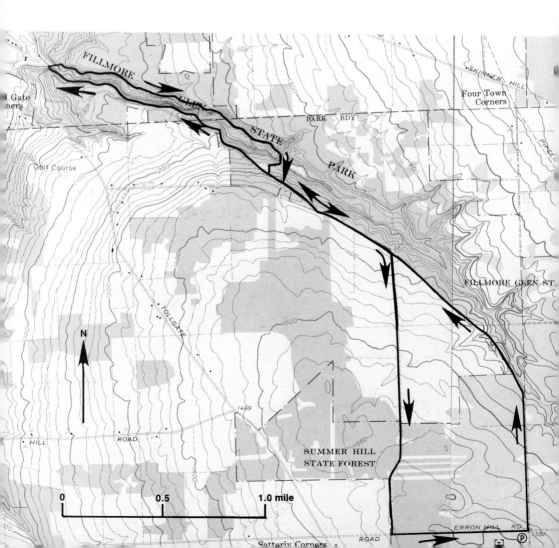

Locke. Turn left on NY 90 and drive east for 4.4 miles to Lick Street, a dirt road on the left. Turn here and drive north for 1.5 miles to the first intersection. Turn left here onto another dirt road (this is Hoag Avenue, which becomes Erron Hill Road at the next crossroad, but there is no sign at this corner). Drive west 1.1 miles to where Hoag Avenue intersects a north-south jeep trail. Park your vehicle here.

Trail. You are now in the midst of Summer Hill State Forest. Start your hike by walking north on the jeep trail. Shortly you come to a clearing on the right in a stand of hardwoods, mostly maples. For those planning a weekend of hiking here, this might be a good spot to set up camp.

Beyond this point the road becomes more narrow and less used. Within ¼ mile you will notice that the ground becomes wet and boggy; this is a drainage area that feeds the brook flowing into Fillmore Glen. In the next ¼ mile, the jeep trail gives way to a single lane that leads down a short slope to a narrow footbridge across the brook. Along this trail small orange or yellow plastic markers are nailed to trees, indicating that this is a snowmobile trail in the winter.

Once you reach the footbridge, retrace

Stream running through gorge

your steps uphill for about 50 yards. Look for a small trail on your right (west). This is actually a deer trail that is hard to find when the weeds begin to grow tall. At this point, whether you find the trail or not, climb the embankment through the trees to the top. Here an abandoned road runs parallel to the one you took to the footbridge. Although it is leaf-strewn and weed-covered, this road is easy to find.

Turn right onto the abandoned road as it turns north a short distance, and then west, following the contour of the gully on your right. You are now bushwhacking your way along the gully that represents the southern edge of Fillmore Glen State Park. In about 100 yards, the abandoned road reaches a point where the forest opens up into fields to the east; this marks the end of Summer Hill State Forest and the beginning of Fillmore Glen State Park.

Using the fields as a guide, it is an easy matter to walk the forest edge for the next ¾ mile. You cross two gullies before you intercept a dirt road that bends off to the south and west. Running north from this bend is a snowmobile trail that you may wish to follow down to Fillmore Glen Brook.

Follow the dirt road west for ½ mile, until you reach another road forking to the right. Across this road is a large log to serve as a barrier to all motorized vehicles. Follow this road, which leads in a little over ¼ mile to a paved road. To your right a footpath takes you along the southern rim of Fillmore Glen, which has now turned into a deep ravine on your right.

Follow the path westward until it descends to a picnic area near the park entrance. From the picnic area you can walk upstream a short distance to view the high falls. On your return from the falls, look for a sign directing you up some stone stairs to the gorge trail. This trail takes you past the top of the falls and then along the edge of the stream in the gorge. It is a delightful walk, and the scenery in the gorge is most impressive.

The trail snakes back and forth over footbridges across the stream, and then passes a wide, three-story-high waterfall cascading down the north side of the gorge. About a mile from the picnic area, the trail crosses to the north side of the stream, bringing you to a small lake— actually a manmade impoundment designed to control the water flow through the glen. Follow the footpath around the dam end of the lake, uphill to your right, and onto the paved road you reached earlier. You can now retrace your steps to the dirt road you walked before and to the bend you intercepted when bushwhacking. Turn south (right) at the bend, and follow the dirt road as it rises slightly, giving you a fine view to the west as it passes through open fields.

The road now enters Summer Hill State Forest, passing through a stand of evergreens. One-quarter mile takes you through the neck of this section of forest to Erron Hill Road. Before reaching the road, however, you have an excellent view of the open land as it slopes downward to Owasco Inlet Valley. Thickly forested Jewett Hill rises on the other side. Turn left (east) on Erron Hill Road for the ¾-mile walk through tall evergreens back to your vehicle.

If you are planning a weekend outing in Summer Hill, there are other loops you can walk. One follows the jeep trail you took earlier across Fillmore Glen Brook, then up Sun Lane to Lick Street and back. Still another turns north on Lick Street, runs to Fillmore Road, and then turns north on Dumplin Hill Road to Brockway Road. From here you can walk to Salt Road, which runs south out of Dresserville and back to Fillmore Road, which takes you past the birthplace of Millard Fillmore.

Hewitt State Forest

Total distance: 3 miles
Hiking time: 1½ hours
Vertical rise: 780 feet
Maps: USGS 7½' Homer; USGS 7½' Otisco Valley

Compared to most other state reforestation areas, Hewitt State Forest is small, covering only about two square miles of hardwoods and evergreens. Nevertheless, it is a delight to hike, primarily because you can walk a natural loop in just over an hour and because it is so rarely used. Except during deer hunting season, you will generally have this little forest to yourself.

This area offers some excellent vistas, for it sits astride the highland overlooking Skaneateles Lake to the northwest, Otisco Lake to the north, and the Tully Lakes to the east. If you look northeast from a high point on the northern edge of the forest, you see Preble Hill a mile away and Gifford Hill two miles away, both 1,800 feet high. Two miles to the south is Brake Hill, which, like the crest you are standing on, reaches an elevation of 1,860 feet. Some local people refer to this high point in the state forest as Hewitt Hill, but officially it has no name.

Access. Hewitt State Forest is reached most easily by following NY 41 to the village of Scott, which is 9 miles north of Homer and 20 miles south of Skaneateles. At the crossroads in the center of

Scott, head north on NY 41 for 0.9 mile to arrive at Hewitt Road, on your right. Turn here and head east. A few hundred feet from NY 41, you pass over Grout Brook, which flows south through Scott and beyond before turning north to empty into Skaneateles Lake. It is one of the famous trout streams of central New York; during spring, rainbow trout leave the lake and swim up the brook to spawn.

After crossing Grout Brook, Hewitt Road becomes a two-lane, hard-packed dirt road. Drive one mile to the first crossroad, turn right, and drive south 0.7 mile. Here you will see a little-used jeep trail entering the forest on your left. Park your vehicle by the side of the road and begin your walk.

Trail. Enter the woods, following the jeep trail due east. This trail is unmarked, and although the forest is not large you should bring a compass and map. For nearly ¼ mile you walk a course due east past an old stone fence, a reminder that this area was once farmland, perhaps as recently as 50 to 75 years ago, when the fields were divided by fences made of stones unearthed during spring plowing. The trail you are walking is an abandoned wagon road, which now turns to your right. After a short distance it turns left, heading you gradually downhill in an easterly direction.

In another hundred feet or so, the trail turns left (north); in five minutes you find it bending slightly to the right, taking you downhill on a northeasterly course. You continue the descent until you cross a small brook, where you turn sharply right. Here the trail begins to arc in a half circle before straightening out to head in a northeasterly direction. The descent now becomes more pronounced. Through the trees ahead you will see signs of a single-lane dirt road, on which you emerge a few minutes later.

Callan Creek, which is one of the headwaters of the West Branch of the Tioughnioga River, begins at the top of Hewitt Hill and flows southeast beside the dirt road on which you are now standing. In 1½ miles it reaches Cold Brook, which in turn flows into the West Branch just south of Little York Lake.

Turn left on the dirt road and walk north. This part of the hike is most pleasant, for the road is canopied by trees, providing a welcome shade on a sunny day. One-half mile along the way a road turns off to the left. Actually, this is a short loop that takes you down to the creek and then back to the road; so it is a nice place to stop for a break.

When you have rested, continue northward on the dirt road for another ½ mile, where you intersect a hard-packed, two-lane dirt road. You are back on Hewitt

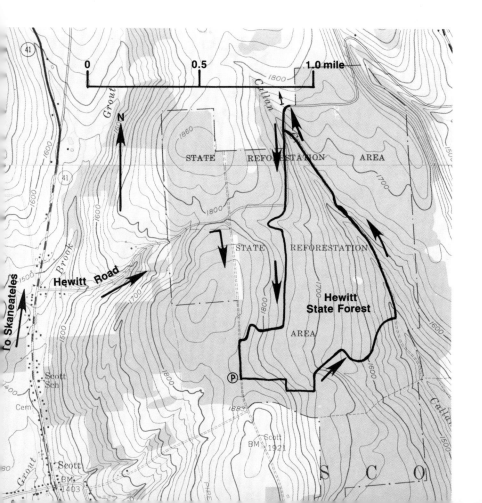

Road. Turn right and walk a short distance to the end of the forest plantation. You are now overlooking open fields; to the northeast you can see Preble Hill and Gifford Hill.

Retrace your steps to continue on the two-lane dirt road for about ¼ mile. Just before it turns sharply to the right a jeep trail enters the forest, straight ahead heading south. Take this trail. After several hundred feet, it turns right and then swings around a gully before again turning south. From this point on the trail runs straight for a little over ½ mile and then turns sharply right. After another five minutes walking, you emerge from the woods onto the road on which your vehicle is parked. Turn left to return to your vehicle parked ¼ mile down the road.

During your hike you are likely to see many deer tracks on the trail. Hewitt provides good cover, food, and protection to the local deer herd, which can travel south beyond the state land through heavy wood cover west of the hamlet of East Scott. This provides them a sizable range. You also may notice raccoon tracks, particularly near the little streams and creeks, for Hewitt State Forest has an abundant supply of small game in addition to its deer herd. If you walk carefully and quietly, you may even see some wildlife.

This highland area catches the snow from the north, and the forest provides good cover so the snow packs well and stays long. The route described is ideal for snowshoeing and Nordic skiing; the trails and roads are wide enough to give the snowshoer or skier adequate room for maneuvering. Hewitt Road is plowed in the winter, giving you direct access to the state forest.

Heiberg Memorial Forest

Total distance: 5 miles
Hiking time: 2½ hours
Vertical rise: 1,932 feet
Maps: USGS 7½′ Tully; USGS 7½′ Truxton

"Variety" is probably the best single word to describe the Heiberg Forest area, for here you will find a diverse network of trails, fire lanes, and dirt roads to hike, as well as many vistas and overlooks and an assortment of ponds that hold numerous species of gamefish. You will also find a self-guided nature trail that is a delight to walk, and a series of trails that lead you through large stands of hardwoods and into the territory of several herds of white-tailed deer. From here you may emerge into an area of thick overgrowth, the ideal habitat of the ruffed grouse for which this forest is well known. There is even a relatively large tract (off-limits) set aside to study the black-tailed deer, imported from Utah, and a pond used to observe the feeding behavior of the rainbow trout.

The 3,780-acre Heiberg Memorial Forest is located atop Truxton Hill (el. 2,020 feet), a wide, flat ridge that overlooks the towns of Tully to the north and Truxton to the southwest. At first glance, it looks like many other state reforestation areas—but a bit tidier, perhaps. The difference is in its use, for this is an outdoor classroom and experimental station used by the State University of New York College of Environmental Science and Forestry. Offi-

cially it is designated as the "Tully Campus, Heiberg Memorial Forest." Still, the touches of civilization here are few, in the forms of the resident forest manager's home and adjacent truck garage and, further down the road, a small house with several outbuildings that provide shelter for the western black-tailed deer.

Hiking in Heiberg Forest, you are walking through biological time and succession as the land returns to its natural state. First settled by pioneers in the late 1700s, the area developed from virgin forest into farmland. However, the soil proved to be highly acidic and poorly drained, and by the 1840s the farmers had turned to lumbering to supplement their incomes and supply the railroad's growing demand for fuel. This only added to the region's economic difficulties, as quality timber soon became scarce and fast water runoff on the naked land made farming more and more unfeasible. Between 1870 and 1925, two-thirds of the population left the area, and the fields that had been so painfully cleared began to revert to hardwoods. Conifers were planted later when the state began to purchase land in the 1930s.

As you walk, look about for evidence

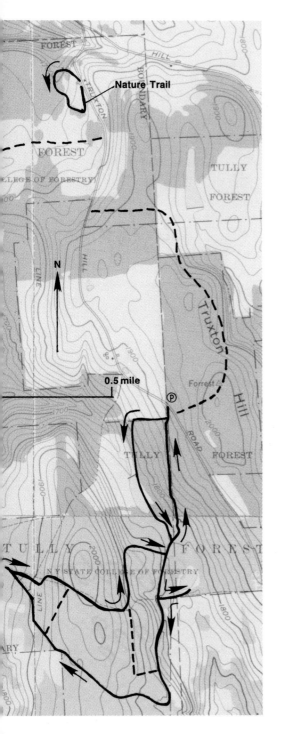

of the succession from wilderness to farmland to wilderness. You may find old stone fences running through the forest, traces of old wagon roads, barbed wire embedded in old trees, and mature forest in areas where crops once grew.

Access. Heiberg Forest and Truxton Hill can be reached from Tully, south of Syracuse and just off I-81. From the center of Tully drive east on NY 80 for a mile, and turn right onto Railroad Street. At the end of the block, bear left and then right across the railroad tracks onto Grove Street, which at the village edge changes to West Hill Road. Continue uphill on West Hill Road for 1.8 miles. When you reach the hilltop, look back. You have a fine vista of Tully village, the wide, north-south Tully valley, and the Tully Lakes, a cluster of large and small "kettle lakes" formed by the retreating glacier thousands of years ago.

Here also a dirt road, Maple Ridge Road (Truxton Hill Road on the USGS map) forks to the right, and a sign on the left informs you that you are entering Heiberg Forest. In 0.3 mile you come to a sign on your right announcing the Nature Trail, which you can walk on your own. Another 0.4 mile brings you to a sign for Pond 1; the ½-mile lane to the pond also makes a pleasant walk. Continue another 0.7 mile down Maple Ridge Road, past the sheds housing the black-tailed deer and the forest manager's house to a fork. On your left is a small parking area; leave your vehicle here.

Trail. Start your hike by following the right fork for 100 feet to a sign pointing to Pond 3. Pick up the footpath by the sign, and follow it downhill past a large stand of white cedar. At the base of the hill, the trail turns left, running along the forest edge for ¼ mile. On your right are open fields; ahead you can see Pond 3, which is stocked with rainbow trout. You

Heiburg

may fish here, but you must obtain a permit from the forest manager, because the pond is a research site. You will find the rainbows big and sassy whether you fly fish or spin cast.

Continue past the pond to a dirt road. Turn right, and walk south about ½ mile to a sign that points to Pond 2, a short walk away. All Heiberg's ponds are open to fishing. They are also used by deer as watering holes and by ducks and geese in the fall as resting and feeding places.

Return to the dirt road, and continue walking south, heading uphill. At the top of the climb, you have an overlook to the south. The road now bends to the right, gradually arcing to the west and then the north. A mile from the overlook the road starts to descend. On your right is an unmarked fire lane. Bear right onto the fire lane, which runs straight in a southeast direction for ¼ mile, turns left and then right, and again heads in a straight line downhill. Halfway down it intersects an-

other fire lane. Turn left here and follow the fire lane. In ½ mile it turns and heads downhill to intersect the road you walked earlier. The walk through this section of Heiberg is most pleasant. The fire lanes are broad, clean, and canopied by tall trees. When you reach the dirt road, turn left and walk back to your vehicle. On both sides of the road are stately cedars that give a special charm to this last stretch. The road ascends gradually and then flattens out as you near your vehicle.

This also is great ski touring country. The terrain is varied, with small hills and level stretches—just the kind of landscape ski tourers love—and the snow comes early, packs well, and stays deep. The forest is laced with ski touring trails, and there are miles of woodland trails for the snowshoer to walk. Maple Ridge Road is plowed as far as the forest manager's house, giving you easy access to all the key trails.

10

Highland Forest

Total distance: 4½ miles
Hiking time: 2½ hours
Vertical rise: 1,160 feet
Maps: USGS 7½′ DeRuyter; Park Map

This 2,700-acre county park sits astride Arab Hill (el. 1,940 feet) in the high land south of Syracuse. As you enter the park, and just before reaching the parking lot, you are treated to a vista of rolling hills, woodlands, and farmlands, for Highland Forest is the high point of the region, overlooking the lower lands to the north.

With its almost Adirondack-like appearance and its network of walking trails, fire lanes, and truck trails, Highland Forest is ideal for the hiker. As it is popular for horseback riding, the county maintains riding trails and provides a corral. Near the parking lot there are facilities for picnicking and a softball diamond. During the winter months the forest is a mecca for cross-country skiers, for it offers some of the finest maintained public trails in central New York.

The Onondaga County Parks and Recreation Department has developed an excellent system of hiking trails in this large forest tract. Highland boasts four hiking trails that begin and end at the parking lot at the northern end of the forest. The "A" loop is just short of a mile long and takes only 30 minutes to walk. The "B" loop runs just over a mile and takes 40 minutes; the "C" loop, at 2¾ miles, takes 1½ hours, and the Main Trail, at 8¼

miles, takes 4 to 5 hours. The forest also has a number of interconnected jeep trails, truck trails, and fire lanes so the enterprising day hiker can make up an endless variety of hikes to suit particular interests and timetables.

The route presented here travels for some distance on each of the four maintained hiking trails and on some of the many jeep and truck trails. This is a day-use area, so don't plan on camping out. Overnight camping is restricted to organized groups, such as the Scouts, and only then by reservation. If you alter the route described here, be sure to return to your car before dark.

Access. Highland Forest is located south of Syracuse and east of Tully, just off NY 80. From the village of Fabius, travel east on NY 80 for 2.2 miles until you see a Highland Forest sign on the left that directs you to the right onto the paved Highland Park Road. After making the turn, drive uphill for 1.1 miles to the parking area on your right, opposite a cluster of buildings: the Community House (in winter a warming hut for cross-country skiers), the park office, and the Pioneer Museum, housing a collection of farm implements, home furnishings, books, and

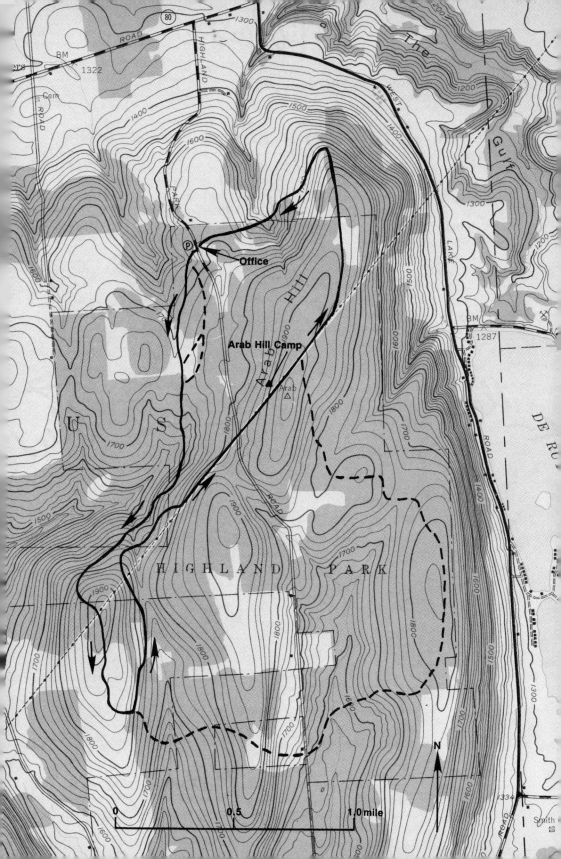

other items of rural life in Onondaga County in the 1800s and early 1900s.

Trail. The trailhead is on the far side of the parking area, next to an information booth and map board. At the park office, you can obtain both a mimeographed guide to the "A" loop, which doubles as a nature trail, and a scaled contour map, showing all the trails, roads, and fire lanes. The trail system is well-marked; look for the stylized yellow pine tree design painted on trees.

Starting at the information booth, you enter the woods on the "A" loop and cross a footbridge over one of the several small brooks you come to on your hike; together these streams make up the headwaters of the Tioughnioga River, which flows south through Cortland and Binghamton to the Susquehanna River.

Beyond the bridge, the trail winds through hardwood trees for ¼ mile and enters an evergreen stand. This is a good place to test your skill at tree identification, so bring your field guide. Many of the trees throughout the forest are man-planted, and the variety is most impressive. Among the evergreens are red, white, Ponderosa, pitch, jack, sugar, and lodgepole pine; white, Norway, Engleman, and blue spruce; Douglas and balsam fir; and white cedar. Among the hardwoods are American basswood, quaking aspen, white ash, black cherry, yellow birch, American beech, paper birch, sugar maple, northern red oak, and red maple.

View from Highland Forest

A short distance into the evergreens, you reach a set of signs; two point left for the Nature Trail and Picnic Area, and one points right for the Main Trail. The "A" loop returns to the parking area by way of the Nature Trail.

You continue on the Main Trail. In about 400 feet a sign points left to the "B" loop, which also returns directly to the parking area. Stay on the Main Trail. A few hundred feet further, you cross a dirt road and enter a stand of white and red pines, which soon gives way to hardwoods.

The trail now runs due south, parallel to a gully on your left, which becomes deeper as you walk south. After a mile, the trail begins to descend more steeply, finally turning left into the gully at a point where two brooks merge. After swinging back and forth across the water three times on footbridges, the trail winds up a slight incline to intersect a truck trail.

Bear left on the truck trail, still heading uphill. By now you have passed over an area that 50 years ago was farmland. In 1930 the county acquired its first parcel of land from two farmers, and with that purchase Highland Forest was founded. During the next three years of the Great Depression, the county obtained nine more farms, and by 1935 it had acquired two additional parcels to make up 90 percent of what is now the forest.

You soon reach a sign marking the place where the "C" loop and the Main Trail diverge. The "C" loop continues on the truck road, but the Main Trail, which is still your route, heads to the right and downhill into a gully. The small brook at the bottom drops into a much deeper ravine on your right.

Here a sign points right to Easy Street and left to Goat Trail. Unless you like hard climbing, stay on Easy Street, which swings right out of the gully and makes a sharp left up a moderate ¼-mile incline. At the top, the trail takes you out of the woods, across a powerline right-of-way, and back into the forest again. The trail levels out 1,000 feet beyond the right-of-way, and a sign informs you that you have reached the highest point in the forest, 1,940 feet.

You soon begin a gradual descent. The trail, here a truck road, bends left (east) and shortly encounters a jeep trail with a marker on the right-hand corner. (The jeep and truck trails are numbered, not named.) The corner marker has two numbers: 27, which is the road you have been walking, and 25, which runs in front of you. An arrow also points left to the park office. Following the arrow, keep left on Road 25 for 1,500 feet until it intersects Road 29. Turn left and head uphill; in ¼ mile it brings you back to the powerline right-of-way. Cross it and re-enter the woods, where you will see another sign to the Goat Trail. Take this trail, which leads downhill to the brook you crossed earlier. Retrace your route to the truck road, turn right and walk about 50 feet to the powerline cut. You are now back on the "C" loop.

The hike continues, however, to the right up the truck trail. When you come to the Arab Hill Camp, go around a road barrier, and head uphill for ¼ mile, where you intersect another stretch of the Main Trail, which has been running north on Road 5. At this point, the Main Trail turns off Road 5 to follow the powerline for about 1,000 feet before bearing left into the forest again. Stay on the Main Trail, which now runs north for ½ mile and then loops back, running southwest for ¼ mile and then due west for another ¼ mile, bringing you back to the park office and your start.

This area is a ski tourer's delight. There are four groomed and maintained trails designed for novice through advanced, and the snows come early and stay late—usually into the end of March.

11

Morgan Hill State Forest

Total distance: 9½ miles
Hiking time: 5 hours
Vertical rise: 1,988 feet
Map: USGS 7½' Tully

Like the persons for whom they were named, Fellows Hill, Jones Hill, and Morgan Hill are next door neighbors. Spread over these three hills, all about 2,000 feet in elevation, are 5,508 acres of state land, making a varied hiking terrain. Officially, this area is called Morgan Hill State Forest, although locally it is known variously as Fabius Forest, Morgan Hill, or Shackham Woods.

Through this state land and over some adjoining private land runs the Onondaga Trail. Designed, marked, and maintained by members of the Onondaga Chapter of the Adirondack Mountain Club, it is one of the spur trails to the Finger Lakes Trail (FLT) system. The trail is well groomed and marked with orange blazes painted on trees.

The entire Morgan Hill State Forest area is covered with trees,with about 70 percent in pine and spruce plantations and the other 30 per cent natural hardwoods. In the middle of the forest there is even a section of virgin timber several hundred years old. You will find some fine overlooks here, as well as magnificent Tinker Falls, a pond stocked with brook trout, a lean-to, a rushing wilderness brook, and a series of hills, gullies, and ravines to add variety to your hike.

The area in and around Morgan Hill State Forest also displays a variety of landmarks produced by the several ice sheets that once covered New York—a kettle lake, a through valley, a hanging falls, and outwash hummocks. In short, the Morgan Hill area is a hiker's delight.

Access. You begin your hike on the Onondaga Trail at Spruce Pond, a small impoundment just 0.2 mile southwest of Fellows Hill. (The pond is not shown on the USGS map as it was created after the map was last updated.)

Spruce Pond, in turn, can be reached from I-81 by exiting at Tully (about halfway between Syracuse and Cortland) and then heading east on NY 80. Just beyond the hamlet of Apulia, look for Herlihy Road, a hard-packed, two-lane dirt road. Turn right onto it; in 1.2 miles you reach Morgan Hill State Forest, marked by the end of farm fields and the beginning of woods.

From this point another 0.7 mile brings you to a fork. Take the one-lane dirt road to your right and drive 0.1 mile past a stand of evergreens to a parking area by the dam at the south end of Spruce Pond. Leave your car here.

You will notice that this area is used for

picnicking and camping. If your interests include fishing, you can try the pond for the beautiful red-spotted brook trout stocked by the state.

Trail. On a tree near the parking area is painted the word "Hike" and an arrow pointing across the dam. On the other side, a second sign indicates the beginning of the trail. Follow the trail halfway around the pond and then to the left up a relatively short but steep hill.

Where the orange-marked trail reaches the crest it flattens out and heads west. In about five minutes you start a gradual descent that brings you to a large stand of smooth-barked beeches. Beyond this

point the trees become smaller and gradually thin out as you enter what was once a field, now taken over by saplings and evergreens. From here you are hiking on private land for the next mile.

You soon leave the field and enter a stand of trees that shades an unused wagon trail and a small brook that flows southward to Tinker Falls. After crossing the brook, you pass through another abandoned field before re-entering the woods. The trail wanders a bit here and then brings you to the summit of Jones Hill (el. 1,964 feet).

Your path now descends sharply for about 100 feet. To your immediate right an opening through the trees offers you

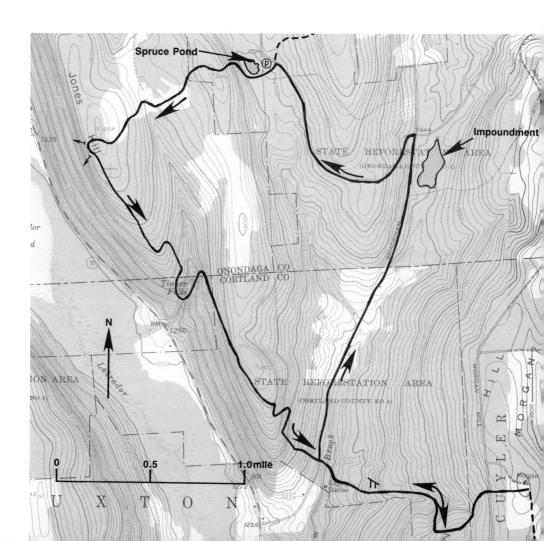

the first vista—a grand view of Labrador Hollow. The Hollow is an excellent example of what geologists call a "through valley"—a valley gouged out by advancing glaciers which overran New York state several times during the Pleistocene epoch, with the last period of glaciation climaxing about 12,000 years ago. Also notice the distinctive U-shape of the valley, another sign of the work done by the advancing glaciers.

The drop-off at the overlook is an abrupt and breathtaking 700 feet. Below you lies the half-mile-long Labrador Pond, a "kettle" lake left behind by the retreating glacier. It is tucked in a narrow valley between Jones and Labrador Hills. A little to your right, Labrador Hollow fans out to the north around and beyond the hamlet of Apulia Station. Still further north, you see a series of smaller hills covered with crop fields and pastureland.

The trail continues for about a mile along the ridge of Jones Hill before beginning a slight descent to a brook. In early spring this brook is high, but by midsummer it may be nothing more than a trickle. Turn right and follow the path to Tinker Falls, where the water plunges some 20 feet off a limestone ledge. This is a "hanging falls," created when the glaciers produced and then deepened the through valley that is now Labrador Hollow. Tinker Falls is a pleasant sight at all times, but most impressive in spring when the brook is running heavy with meltwater.

From Tinker Falls continue south along the ridge for another ½ mile. You now begin a descent, with the trail switching back and forth until it emerges on Shack-

ham Road, a well-maintained, two-lane dirt road 470 feet below the ridge crest. The trail crosses this road and drops sharply for 80 feet to Shackham Brook, a picture-book scene in spring and early summer when its water flows over rocks and boulders, forming riffles and small pools en route through the ravine past large stands of pines and hardwoods. Cross the brook, and follow the trail along the edge of the ravine on your right. You climb fairly steeply for a little better than ½ mile, at which point you come to a lean-to and a stone fireplace. This is an ideal place to stop for a breather. If you are planning a camping trip, the lean-to can be your overnight shelter.

Continue uphill for another ¼ mile to Morgan Hill Road, a one-lane dirt road. Follow the trail across the road about 800 feet to the firetower (no longer in use). You are now at the summit of Morgan Hill (el. 2,000 feet), an excellent place to relax in the shade of the hardwoods and evergreens that surround the tower.

Retrace your steps across Morgan Hill Road and downhill past the lean-to to Shackham Road. Turn right and continue north for 2 miles to the first intersection.

Here Herlihy Road crosses Shackham Road. Through the trees on your right, you see a small pond, a manmade impoundment that is large enough to bring canoeists here for an afternoon of paddling. Turn left onto Herlihy Road and head uphill. After a gentle climb of ¼ mile, the road flattens out, and it is an easy 1½-mile hike back to Spruce Pond and your car.

Susquehanna Hills

12

Shindagin Hollow State Forest

Total distance: 3½ miles
Hiking time: 2 hours
Vertical rise: 510 feet
Map: USGS 7½' Speedsville

Shindagin Hollow is a long north-south valley, almost gorgelike in its narrowness, located ten miles southeast of Ithaca and Cayuga Lake. It was once the route of a well-used Indian trail that ran northeast from the main Cayuga-Owego trail to what is now the village of Caroline, where it met another heavily-traveled Indian route, the Onondaga-Owego trail. Today this valley sits in the heart of the large parcel of state land called Shindagin Hollow State Forest.

Running in an east-west direction through the forest and across the hollow is the well-marked Caroline section of the main Finger Lakes Trail (FLT), maintained by the Cayuga Trails Club. Using portions of this trail and taking advantage of the network of dirt roads that laces the state forest and adjoining lands, it is possible to devise several delightful loops that will take you through wildernesslike stretches of forest, into deep ravines and narrow valleys, and over open high spots where you can see miles of the surrounding countryside. The entire area is situated on a high tableland averaging about 1,500 feet above sea level. The scenic

Group of hikers in Shindagin

variety found in the forest makes this one of the most attractive sections of the FLT.

While the hiking loop recommended here is relatively short (3½ miles), it gives you a good sample of the region's charm, covering some open highland with views to the north and east, a part of the narrow Shindagin Hollow, and a deep ravine that the FLT follows along its eastern rim to the Shindagin Hollow lean-to.

The lean-to is a good place to spend the night if you would like to cover more territory and explore other sections of the FLT. A ½ mile south of the starting point for this hike, on South Road, the FLT continues east through Potato Hill State Forest. Continuing northward, you arrive at the region's highest point at Padlock Lookout Tower (el. 1,900 feet), where you can see 20 to 30 miles in all directions. You can also follow the FLT to the west out of Shindagin Hollow, across Willseyville Creek in the adjoining valley, and into another unusually attractive region where you will enter Danby State Forest (see Hike 13).

Whatever your preference, you are walking in one of the most heavily forested areas in central New York. With its rolling hills and lush valleys, it is a delight to the eye and a treat for the hiker.

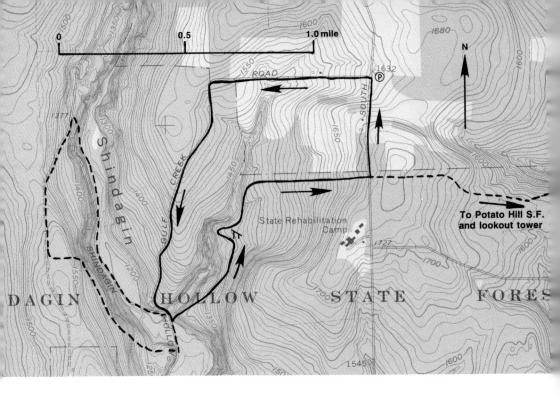

Access. To reach the trailhead from Ithaca, drive east on NY 79 for five miles to NY 330, which forks to your right. Continue on NY 330 another five miles until you intersect Old Seventysix Road at the junction called Guide Board Corners. Turn left onto this road, and drive 2.4 miles to the hamlet of Caroline Center.

If you are approaching from I-81, exit at Whitney Point, and follow NY 79 west 21 miles. Look for Old Seventysix Road on your left just beyond the village of Slaterville Springs; once on Old Seventy-six Road, drive to Caroline Center.

In Caroline Center, turn south onto South Road, a two-lane hard-packed dirt road. Drive 1.2 miles to Gulf Creek Road on your right. Park your vehicle at the intersection.

Trail. Start your hike by walking west on Gulf Creek Road, which runs through open fields, giving you a good view of

the countryside to the north and west. For the next ½ mile the road descends gradually, crossing a trickle of a brook (in spring), and then begins a short ascent to the forest edge. You are now entering the northern section of Shindagin Hollow State Forest at one of the high spots of the region (el. 1,550 feet).

A short distance into the forest, the road turns sharply left and heads south. Within several hundred feet it begins the descent into Shindagin Hollow. It is a 4 mile walk from the road's turn to the bottom of the hollow; about halfway down the road pitches downward more sharply, with the slope becoming more pronounced as you near the bottom. The trees along the road provide cool shade during the summer.

At the bottom, Gulf Creek Road intersects Shindagin Hollow Road. You are now in a narrow ravine with forested sides that rise sharply almost 350 feet.

Flowing through the hollow is Shindagin Hollow Creek.

Turn left onto Shindagin Hollow Road and follow it south for about 100 feet. To your left you will see a cut into the side of the hill. It is the outlet of a deep, narrow gorge; the FLT follows its eastern rim. During the early spring as the snow waters roar down the mile-long gorge, you are treated to an impressive sight here. At the outlet, just before the spot where the waters pour into the Shindagin Hollow Creek, there is a narrow cut in the shale rock. As the waters rush through this cut each spring, they form a raging cataract. Shindagin is a corruption of the Indian word Shandaken, meaning "rapid water." It may have been here during the spring run-offs that the Indians watched the torrential waters of the gorge meeting those of Shindagin Hollow Creek and spoke of the place as Shandaken.

A few feet south of this point on Shindagin Hollow Road, a white FLT marker directs you across the creek (during the summer and fall it is a dry stream bed) to an abandoned road. Follow this road uphill. The initial climb of several hundred feet is quite steep, but soon the road levels out. After a gentle ½-mile climb, the trail turns sharply to your left and begins a gradual downward pitch. Within a short distance the trail flattens.

To your left is a thirty-foot drop into a ravine; ahead and a little to your right is the Shindagin Hollow lean-to. The hemlocks surrounding it make this a most inviting place to stop for a break or to stay overnight.

Follow the white blazes of the FLT as they take you north past the lean-to. The trail snakes through the forest along the ravine's edge for about ¼ mile, and then it turns right taking you up for ½ mile on a straight easterly course to South Road. Once on South Road, turn north. In less than ½ mile, you are back at your vehicle.

The FLT crosses South Road, and, if you like, you can add a few more miles to your hike by continuing eastward. The trail takes you through a hardwood forest for 1½ miles and eventually across Boyer Creek to the paved highway. Old Seventysix Road. If you stay on the FLT, another mile brings you to the Potato Hill State Forest. The walk through this forest is 2¼ miles long, and another mile to the north brings you to the Padlock Lookout Tower.

Another loop that you may wish to add to the recommended hike follows Shindagin Hollow Road north for a mile. Here a jeep trail forks to the left and runs south, almost paralleling Shindagin Hollow Road. If you follow this jeep trail, you will intersect the east-west FLT. You can then turn left (east) on the FLT and follow it downhill to the hollow and back onto Shindagin Hollow Road.

These hills hold the snow well. Most of the dirt roads in the area are plowed, giving you direct access to the FLT. This section is ideal for cross-country ski enthusiasts as the terrain is just varied enough to make ski touring challenging and interesting.

13

Danby State Forest

Total distance: 9 miles
Hiking time: 4½ hours
Vertical rise: 1,472 feet
Map: USGS 7½' Willseyville

Danby State Forest is a large land tract (7,086 acres) situated 14 miles south of Ithaca. It occupies the highland region just south of NY 96B, a highway that runs southeast from Ithaca to Owego, passing through the hamlet of Danby, from which the state forest derives its name. This high area is tableland, a rolling, wooded landscape mixed with open fields. It is uncommonly picturesque, especially in late spring or early summer when the valleys are carpeted in deep green and the hilltops are still dressed in softer, yellow-green.

Essayist and naturalist Hal Borland wrote that "half the benefit, and even more of the satisfaction, of walking comes from the leisurely change of scene." In Danby, there is always a leisurely change of scene. Here you find long fields as well as deep woods, tree-lined lanes as well as meandering foot-trails passing through forest glens and sun-washed glades, and with each new turn comes a change in mood. You can walk for literally miles without seeing any houses, farms, or people, and yet this sense of remoteness is complemented by a feeling of openness that results from the many overlooks where the surrounding hilltops and valleys spread out before you.

Danby State Forest is a long swath of land bounded on the west by Michigan Hollow, on the north by Danby Creek Valley, and on the east by Willseyville Valley. The distinctive geological characteristic of the region is its sharply pointed hilltops with steep sides and narrow valleys, which make the landscape look more rugged and mountainous than it actually is. Most of the hills barely rise over 1,600 feet, yet they seem much higher.

Through the area, this run of eight miles of Finger Lakes Trail (FLT), was built and is currently maintained by the Cayuga Trails Club, one of the several sponsoring groups of the Finger Lakes Trail Conference.

Michigan Hollow takes its name from early settlers who started for Michigan but decided to stay here instead, giving the area the name of their once hoped-for destination. Geologically, the hollow straddles a divide, where water flows from one pond northward to form Buttermilk Creek, which eventually empties into Cayuga Lake, and from another pond southward to form Michigan Creek, which flows to the Susquehanna River.

Hiker studies map in Danby State Forest

Willseyville Valley and nearby Danby Creek Valley are what geologists call "through valleys," carved by glaciers that deepened the valleys and steepened the hillsides. The east side of Eastman Hill is a good example of such oversteepening, with a drop of 700 feet into Willseyville Valley at about a 35-degree angle.

Willseyville Valley is also known as the "Warrior's Trail." This was the main Indian Trail from Cayuga Lake to the Susquehanna River, and the route taken by the

Indians and Tories in 1779 during the Revolutionary War to harass troops of the Continental Army seeking to join the Sullivan Expedition. The first settlers who came to Ithaca from Owego in 1789 used this trail, widening it for their ox carts.

The hike recommended here runs eastward over the highest point of the region, downhill, and up again to the top of Eastman Hill. With several substantial climbs it is a moderate-to-difficult hike, but the effort is worth it.

Access. The trailhead can be reached by taking NY 96B south from Ithaca 6.4 miles to Danby. Continue through Danby another 2.6 miles to paved South Danby Road on your right. This road can also be reached from the south by taking NY 96B; then drive north through Willseyville for 4.5 miles to South Danby Road, on your left.

Once on South Danby Road, drive south 1.5 miles, and watch for white blazes on both sides of the road that indicate where the FLT crosses. The first blaze is on the right. Drive beyond it over a small brook (Miller Creek) for 225 feet. Another FLT marker can now be seen on your left. Park here.

Trail. Follow the FLT uphill to the east; in several hundred feet you reach an abandoned road by that runs due east. The FLT, marked by white blazes, follows this road steadily uphill for almost a mile through thick woods, mostly pine and hemlock. As you near the top of the hill, the ascent becomes more moderate, and

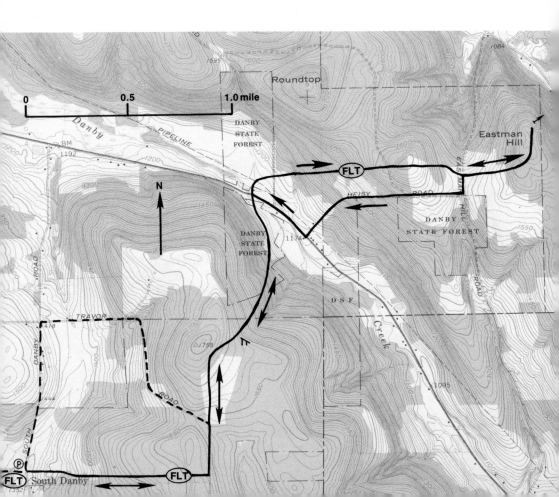

the trail finally levels out as you pass through a stand of pines just before reaching Travor Road.

Turn left and follow this dirt lane northward for about ¼ mile until it bends to the left. Here the FLT leaves Travor Road and continues north along an old farm road past a cellar hole. Shortly the trail takes you into a stand of larches, where it bends to the right, moving through a small clearing, and then turns left (north) into another larch plantation. For the last ¼ mile you have been making a moderate ascent. You now are almost at the highest point in the region, (el. 1,758 feet); this unnamed hilltop is in the woods just off to your left. A little farther along, a spur trail bears off to the right about 100 feet to the Tamarack lean-to, a delightful place to spend the night.

Just beyond the spur trail, the main trail pitches downward. The hill here is quite steep; in less than ¾ mile you descend 584 feet. En route you pass a second spur trail that goes south about 100 feet to a spring. Continue downhill through the woods until you emerge in an open area; turn left for a short distance and continue until you reach a small stream (Danby Creek) at the base of the hill. Just ahead is NY 96B, and across Danby Creek Valley you see a cluster of hilltops: Durfee Hill, Roundtop, and Eastman Hill.

Follow the creek a short distance to a culvert and NY 96B. Cross the highway, and pick up the white blazes on the other side. Soon you encounter a fence, which you follow for about 100 feet to enter an open field. Across the field you can see a white blaze painted on a stick. Follow the trail to this point, then cross the rest of the field to the bottom of the hill where the FLT enters the woods and starts uphill on a generally easterly course.

In about ½ mile, the trail leaves the woods and crosses a field, skirting a pond on the left and continuing uphill through a small stand of pines. Here the trail swings left and goes north uphill through an abandoned field. You are now at the top of an unnamed hill, having climbed 476 feet from Danby Creek Valley.

The trail crosses a little-used road and passes through a field containing aspen trees. To your right you have a fine view to the southeast. Follow the trail as it dips down into a shallow, wooded valley, passes through pines, and then heads uphill through a stand of locust trees to emerge on Eastman Hill Road, a dirt lane. Cross the road and continue uphill for about ¼ mile along a hedgerow, then follow an old farm road through a field. You are now on top Eastman Hill (el. 1,690 feet). If you continue a few hundred yards north along the ridge, you should be able to see east through the trees to glimpse Willseyville Valley 595 feet below.

Now retrace your steps to Eastman Hill Road. Turn left (south), and in a short distance you come to Heisy Road, another single-lane dirt road. Turn right (west), and follow Heisy Road downhill to NY 96B where you turn right and walk ¼ mile north to pick up the FLT. You can now retrace your route on the FLT uphill past the lean-to, across Travor Road, and then downhill to your vehicle.

An alternate route back to your vehicle takes you right (northwest) on Travor Road and then west to the intersection with South Danby Road. Turn left (south) here and walk ¾ mile back to your vehicle. This route takes you over a hill and through some fields, offering you delightful views to the north, east, and south. You may lengthen your hike during a weekend outing by following the FLT west from the spot where you parked your vehicle. A three-mile walk brings you to Michigan Hollow, where the FLT crosses Michigan Creek.

14

Beaver Creek State Forest

Total distance: 7½ miles
Hiking time: 4 hours
Vertical rise: 1,060 feet
Map: USGS 7½′ Brookfield

Beaver Creek State Forest extends from Mount Hunger on the west to Witter Hill on the east. Beaver Creek, an attractive and productive small trout stream that gives its name to the state forest, flows south through the long narrow valley that makes up the middle section of the 3,346-acre tract of state land.

The state forest lies 18 miles due south of Utica. A mile from its southern boundary is the village of Brookfield, and four miles from its northern boundary is US 20. You will be hiking in the Susquehanna Hills, which rise out of the Mohawk Valley in the north and level off in the south at an elevation between 1,800 to 2,000 feet.

The highest spot in the area is Witter Hill, at an elevation of 1,900 feet. From the trailhead to the summit, the rise is 500 feet. Topographically, this is high rolling country where, as on Witter Hill, you find hills and valleys on top of the hills themselves. You'll be walking through woods of heavy-boughed conifers and thick-trunked hardwoods that make this a pleasant region for hikers.

Access. The trailhead in the state forest is reached via US 20 in the north. From

Sangerfield at the junction of US 20 and NY 12, drive east 0.6 mile to a road that intersects from the south. A sign here calls it Brookfield Road (elsewhere it is called Beaver Creek Road). Turn right here, and drive 4.5 miles south past Mount Hunger on the right to an intersection with Bliven Road. Turn left on Bliven Road, and drive 0.5 mile to its intersection with the north-south Fairground Road, where you turn right. Drive south another 0.7 mile to a picnic area on your right where there are tables, toilets, and a hitching rail for horses. Park here.

Trail. Your hiking trail consists of several miles of truck roads and horse trails. While the trail system is not marked for hiking, round yellow signs with a horse-head silhouette indicate the route of the bridle paths that you can follow. Beaver Creek is linked to its close neighbor, Baker Memorial State Forest (see Hike 15), by horse trails on which you can walk miles and miles of trails from one state forest to the other.

These groomed and maintained trails start on the west side of Beaver Creek and loop north and then east, taking you over open terrain, across hilltops and into valleys, and then down along the east side of Beaver Creek Valley to the fair-ground just outside the village of Brookfield.

At your starting point at the picnic area, pick up a yellow-marked trail (the width of a lane) heading uphill in a southeastern direction. It is straight and rather steep for the first ¾ mile until you intersect a wider dirt road about 300 feet above your starting point.

Once you turn left on the dirt road, hiking becomes a little easier, even though you are still moving uphill. Just about ½ mile brings you to a lane that forks to the right with a yellow arrow pointing down the path. This will be your exit when you complete the loop in a clockwise fashion, but for now continue north on the dirt road.

Here you are on the north-south ridge

of Witter Hill, about a mile in length. Another ¼ mile uphill brings you to the knob of Witter Hill. You now start a series of short descents and ascents as the road dips and rises in the rolling, forested terrain. In the next ½ mile, you encounter two dips that drop you to an elevation of 1,700 feet before you climb back to 1,800 feet.

As you reach the northern edge of the state forest, the road swings to the right and heads east. For the next 1½ miles it is relatively level. As you hike through the hardwoods, the trees on your right begin to thin out. Suddenly, you look down into a narrow, forested valley about 100 feet below.

Further down the road, an arrow directs you onto a narrower horse trail on your right heading south. The first ½ mile

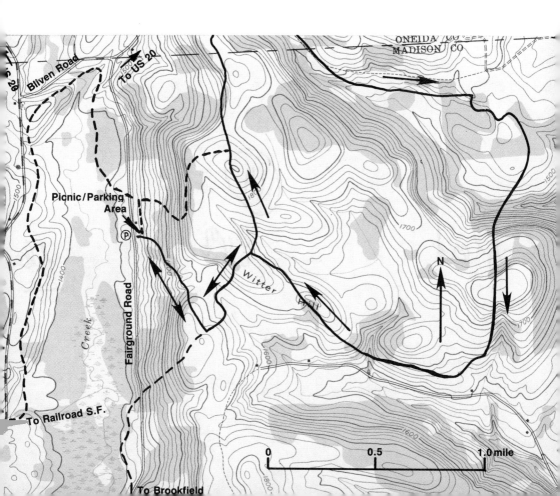

Canopied trail in Beaver Creek State Forest

is fairly flat; the trail begins then to descend, slowly at first and now more steeply as you near the bottom. Your vertical drop is 160 feet in less than ¼ mile.

Next you start an upward climb, a steep ascent of 340 feet. After a brief level stretch on the top, you begin your second—and steeper—descent, which takes you through a stand of spruce trees and down 200 feet. At the bottom, you move through a stand of hardwood and then break out into a large, ½-mile-wide bowl-like valley. This would be a most attractive spot on any trail, but after hiking through miles of forested landscape, you will be especially surprised by the pleasant openness of this hilltop meadow—a change in scenery indeed.

Continue your hike around the southern part of the meadow and back into the forest. You are now walking on the backbone of Witter Hill; the high point in this southern section is 1,740 feet. Another ½ mile brings you to the intersection with the dirt road you hiked earlier. Turn left, and retrace your steps to your vehicle at the picnic area.

You can call it a day. On another day, though, you might follow the yellow-marked bridle path from the picnic area north as it runs parallel with Fairground Road. Soon the trail crosses the road and continues northward on the west side of the road, passing alternately through open stretches and wooded areas.

The trail soon meets Bliven Road and swings west over a small hill, across Beaver Creek, and then over another hill as it enters more open and attractive terrain on its southward journey. You can follow this trail south for several miles and then east for another 1½ miles to enter a second state forest, an 850-acre tract with the odd name of Railroad State Forest. Here you will find a bridle path loop about 3½ miles long.

15

Baker Memorial Forest

Total distance: 13 miles (two days)
Hiking time: 7 hours
Vertical rise: 960 feet
Maps: USGS 7½′ Brookfield; USGS 7½′ Hubbards-
ville; USGS 7½′ Sherburne

This is equestrian country. From a hiker's viewpoint, that's all to the good, for horse trails make excellent hiking trails. If you add the dirt roads, lanes, and snow-mobile trails to the 99-mile horse trail system in the area, you have well over 150 miles of walking trails. That should keep even the most eager and able hiker occupied for a week or more should he or she have a mind to go the whole distance.

This also is picturesque hill country. Topographically, the hills are much more peaked than those further west, a feature that marks them as Susquehanna Hills in contrast to the rounder and flatter Finger Lakes Hills. You will find the skyline angular and irregular and the landscape cleft and rugged-looking—aspects that give this region a special charm.

Officially, this vast state forest (8,070 acres) is named in memory of Charles E. Baker, a regional state forester who was responsible for foresting and developing it into the present multi-use recreation area, but you wouldn't know that from the signs. They read that the land is managed by the state's Department of Environmental Conservation as the "Brookfield Horse Trails: 99 Mile Trail System," one of the largest such systems in the state.

The horse trails not only loop and circle throughout Baker Forest but also connect with those in nearby Railroad State Forest and Beaver Creek State Forest (see Hike 14). They include forested hilltops, open valleys, large ponds, and high ground overlooking Beaver Creek swamp—actually a lush green valley filled with evergreens.

Another of the forest's big assets is the camping area—actually two adjoining areas with picnic tables under shelter and dozens and dozens of well-designed spots for camping and tenting. And it's all free.

Baker Forest merits more than just a day hike. Plan on four or five days, and if you can't manage that, try for at least a long weekend. You can use the camping area as your base while you try the various trails, or you might consider back-packing to the firetower and tenting there, where there is an ideal spot among the evergreens. You'll even find a manmade fireplace for cooking.

All horse trails in Baker Forest are color-coded with red, blue, and yellow discs with a horse head silhouette, so you'll have no difficulty following them. Each main loop is about 33 miles long, and all begin at and return to one Assembly Area. The best way to master the color-coded trail system is to study the map in a free booklet, "Horse Trails in New York State," which you can obtain from the Regional Office, Department of Environmental Conservation, Sherburne, NY 13460.

The marked trails radiate in various directions over Baker's many hills. The extensive forest has three designated high places as well as a number of un-named high spots. Along the forest's northern boundary are, from east to west, ½-mile long Quaker Hill (el. 1,860 feet), mile-long Moscow Hill with a knob at the west rising to 1,740 feet, and Grassy Hill, with two knobs each rising to 1,820 feet.

These are fair-sized hills for this region. Vertical rise from the Assembly Area to the top of Moscow Hill is 300 feet, which gives you a nice steady climb over a half mile.

Access. From the east, Baker Forest can be approached via Skaneateles Turnpike, which begins at NY 8 (running south out of Bridgewater on US 20) and heads west nine miles through Brookfield to West Brookfield, where you drive south

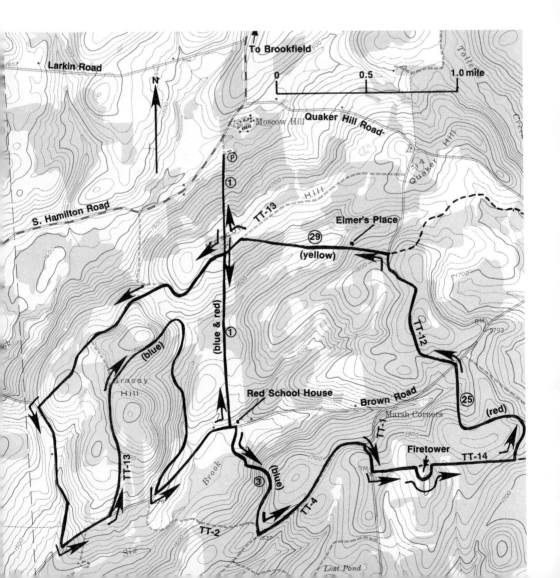

for a mile on South Hamilton Road to the Assembly Area and the trailhead. Or from the west, take NY 12, which runs south out of Utica, crossing US 20 at Sangerfield. From Sangerfield, follow NY 12 south 9.3 miles to East Hamilton. A state sign on the right directs you to "Brookfield Horse Trails." Turn left here onto Larkin Road, and drive one mile to where Crumb Road intersects on the right. Turn south on Crumb Road, and drive 1.4 miles to its intersection with South Hamilton Road. Turn left (east) onto South Hamilton Road, and drive 2.2 miles, where you will see a sign on the right to the Assembly Area. Park here.

Trail. The trailhead is next to the Assembly Area, and to the left is the marked camping area. The starting route (Trail 1) runs south from here to the top of Moscow Hill. We will assume you are tenting near the Assembly Area, so your starting point for each day is at this area.

First Day

Assembly Area to Firetower and back
Distance: 5½ miles
Hiking time: 3 hours
At the Assembly Area, turn onto Trail 1, and head south uphill to the top of Moscow Hill, where you intersect the east-west dirt road, TT-13 (TT stands for truck trail). Here the yellow trail turns left and follows the road. The combined red-and blue-coded horse trail crosses the road and heads into the woods; take this trail.

The narrow trail runs straight south, heading downhill for ¼ mile before leveling off for the next ¼ mile; during the spring you'll encounter a number of soggy spots en route, but higher ground takes you around these. Just beyond the ½-mile mark, the trail rises a bit before starting a downhill descent. As you approach the valley (and another east-west dirt road), the trail crosses a small brook (which eventually feeds into Number Six Brook) before it turns right and comes out on Brown Road.

The trail jogs here. Follow the trail markers by turning left on the road; a short distance up the road, a marker directs you to the right and back into the woods. Just beyond where you turn off the road, you will see on the north side of the road a red building on a small parcel of private land, marked as the Red School House.

Once into the woods, a small sign tells you that this trail is also Trail 3. Soon you cross what is the beginning of Number Six Brook and then start a fairly stiff climb, rising 220 feet in less than ¼ mile before you finally reach a level area. Soon the blue trail comes out on a dirt road; from Brown Road to this one (TT-2 on the map) the distance is just short of a mile.

Continue straight ahead on TT-2 for a short distance to an intersection with TT-4; the blue trail turns right and follows TT-4 southwest. You, however, turn left on TT-4 and follow it uphill for about ¼ mile, where another blue horse trail comes out of the woods and heads northeast on TT-4. Follow the blue markers. A ½ mile further brings you to the intersection with TT-1.

Turn right, and follow TT-1 a short distance to the top of the hill, where an arrow with a red marker directs you to turn left onto another dirt road (TT-14). A ¼ mile hike on this red trail brings you to a fork; follow the right leg, which takes you into an evergreen stand and then to a parkiing area, the highest point in Baker Forest (el. 1,900 feet).

On your left is the firetower, which is no longer used (steps have been removed to prevent people from climbing to the top). Here you'll find some picnic tables and a single fireplace, with plenty

of room for camping. Near the firetower is a boulder with a bronze plaque in memory of Charles E. Baker.

The road on which you came to this site is actually a loop, so follow it back to the red-trail road. Turn right, and continue east on TT-14 and downhill for almost ½ mile, where an arrow directs you to turn left off the road and into the woods. The red trail (Trail 25) now climbs to the top of the hill, levels off for a brief stretch, and then heads downhill, covering a mile before intersecting with Brown Road and TT-12. Follow TT-12 north.

For almost a mile, this shaded road is relatively flat, but then it begins to go downhill. As you near the bottom, a horse trail marked with yellow discs crosses the road (Trail 29). Turn left onto this yellow trail. As you do, you will see a sign on a tree that reads "Elmer's Place."

You are now traveling west. The trail becomes more rocky as it heads downhill, finally crossing a narrow wooden bridge over a small brook. Here you see Elmer's Place, an unoccupied one-room house, on your right. The trail now begins a modest climb until it makes a sharp right-hand turn onto a dirt road (TT-13). Turn left, and follow the dirt road a short distance to a horse trail crossing the road (the trail you walked earlier, Trail 1).

The "Assembly Area" sign directs you right into the woods and downhill. In ½ mile you come to the Assembly Area and your vehicle.

Second Day

Assembly Area to Grassy Hill and back
Distance: 7½ miles
Hiking time: 4 hours

As before, leave the Assembly Area and head to the top of Moscow Hill and the dirt road, TT-13. Turn right onto TT-13.

Horse trail with color markers found in Baker Memorial Forest

Follow the blue markers that take you southwest on TT-13 for a little less than ½ mile to an intersection with another dirt road, forking to the right. Here the blue-coded horse trail (and your route) leaves the road and heads into the woods in a southwesterly direction.

This trail stays in the woods for the next mile as it follows the northwest ridge of Grassy Hill; then it starts to slope downward, descending 100 feet to intersect with a dirt road, Collins Road. At this point, the blue trail turns left and follows Collins Road for almost a mile, where it turns right into the woods. You, however, continue on Collins Road a short distance to the intersection with Brown Road.

Turn left, and follow Brown Road uphill for almost ½ mile to an intersection with TT-13, forking to the left. Take TT-13, and start an uphill climb for a little over ½ mile (an ascent of 160 feet). A southern knob of Grassy Hill lies nearby on your right. A little way further, the blue trail swings back into the woods and climbs a short distance to the northern and second knob of Grassy Hill.

After a short level stretch, the terrain slopes down sharply. The blue trail makes a short descent and then turns right to lead you along the side of the hill in a southernly direction. For the next mile, you follow a level trail, before you make a short descent to exit onto Brown Road.

Turn left, and follow the red-coded Brown Road, which heads downhill, crosses a brook, and levels out; just short of the mile mark, Brown Road intersects with the north-south blue-red horse trail that you walked the day before. Turn left onto this blue-red trail, and head into the woods. Go north uphill and across the brook, and a mile brings you to the top of Moscow Hill and TT-13. Cross the road and make your descent to the Assembly Area.

16

Woodford Memorial Forest

Total distance: 7¼ miles
Hiking time: 4 hours
Vertical rise: 482 feet
Map: USGS 7½' Cassville

What makes this state forest so inviting is its accessibility, easy hiking trails, and an attractive overlook from the area's highest point, Tassel Hill, in the forest's northern section.

Until 1977, the 2,415-acre state forest was known as the Tassel Hill area; when it was officially re-named Albert J. Woodford Memorial Forest, in memory of the district state forester who was responsible for acquiring, reforesting, and developing the land for recreation.

Woodford is south of Utica, between Sangerfield and Bridgewater, in a landform area called Susquehanna Hills. From the Mohawk Valley in the north, the land rises to form the Appalachian highlands of which the Susquehanna Hills are a part. As hills go in this area, Tassel Hill is good-sized, topping out at 1,940 feet. Actually, it is only a bump on the 1½ mile-long ridge that runs north and south through the entire state forest. As the trailhead is at an elevation of 1,557 feet, your vertical ascent is only 383 feet, and you have 3½ miles in which to cover the rise. In short, you climb only 100 feet per mile—something you hardly notice as you hike.

When you reach the summit of Tassel Hill, you share it with a telephone com-

pany microwave tower. Luckily the tower does not obstruct the spectacular vista of the rolling landscape, long ridges, and peaked hilltops to the south and east.

This parcel of state land—3.6 miles long and 3 miles wide—contains two manmade ponds, both at the southern end. The most accessible one is called Chittning Pond. It is easy to reach by a short walk from a parking area just off US 20.

Access. Located off US 20, Woodford can be reached by driving 2.5 miles east of Sangerfield or 5 miles west from the center of Bridgewater. Park off the highway at Janus Road, your trailhead. Janus Road, a dirt truck road, runs in a northeasterly direction from US 20.

Trail. Woodford does not mark any specific foot-trails. You make up your own trail system from existing dirt roads and jeep trails. Some of these are two-lane, others are single-lane, and still others are hardly roads at all.

On Janus Road, the first ½ mile passes through open, field-like landscape. Thereafter, your hiking is in a forest of maple, beech, white ash, and black cherry interspersed with evergreen,

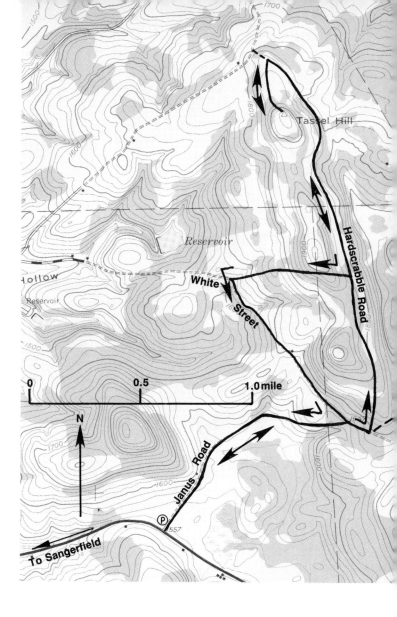

mostly white pine, with some Norway and white spruce. Many of the roads are canopied by hardwood trees that provide welcome shade on a hot, sunny day.

Janus Road pitches down a bit at the start, but then levels off at the 1½-mile mark, where you encounter the northern-bound leg of the V-shaped Hardscrabble Road just a short distance east of the intersection of Janus Road and White Street. At the base of this V, bear left (north) where you find the sharp rise of a small hill. After you have made the 40-foot ascent, the trail levels out to a gradual incline for the next 1¾ miles.

Once you are on the northern leg of Hardscrabble Road, the broad dirt road gives way to a narrow lane. On the left, the forested land rises, climbing over 100 feet to the top of the north-south ridge.

View of Tassel Hill (background) across Chittning Pond in Woodford Memorial Forest

From the intersection at White Street, it is almost a mile to where a narrow lane intersects from the left (that will be the route you take on your return).

Another mile brings you to another road intersecting from the left. This is a southbound road, Tassel Hill Road, which takes you uphill ¼ mile to the summit of Tassel Hill, identified by the microwave tower and the fine view to the south and east. Here's the place to stop, take a lunch break, and enjoy the excellent scenery.

You are now ready for your return hike. Retrace your steps south on Hardscrabble Road to the intersection with the lane mentioned earlier (now on your right); this is just about a mile south of Tassel Hill Road. Turn west onto the lane, climb to the top of the ridge, and continue down the other side to where the lane intersects White Street. This covers just slightly over ½ mile. Turn left (southeast) onto White Street, where a mile walk brings you back to the intersection with Janus Road. Turn right here to return to your parked vehicle on US 20.

17

Taylor Valley State Forest

Total distance: 12 miles (two days)
Hiking time: 6 hours
Vertical rise: 2,120 feet
Maps: USGS 7½′ Cuyler; USGS 7½′ Cincinnatus

For many a hiker, Taylor Valley is the prettiest valley in this general region. The glacier of some 12,000 years ago shaped it; more recently human beings have groomed it, especially in the central section where the valley has been reforested. The glacier-cut of the 12-mile-long valley is what gives it its eye-appeal—a rounded valley floor with steep, almost vertical hillsides.

The central section of the valley is state land and virtually empty of signs of civilization. Nor do you find much by way of farms or hamlets in the southern end. You only begin to see farms when you reach the small hamlet of Cheningo. For the most part, you are surrounded by steep forested hillsides rising 800 feet on both sides of the north-flowing Cheningo Creek.

Taylor Valley State Forest occupies most of the hilltop territory as well. The 4,650-acre state forest spreads from Mount Roderick (el. 1,900 feet) in the southwest to Allen Hill (el. 1,980 feet) in the east and Seacord Hill (el. 1,910 feet) in the northeast.

Through all this state land runs the groomed Finger Lakes Trail (FLT), marked by white blazes on trees. The trail runs six miles from Telephone Road in the south across Taylor Valley Road to end at Cheningo-Solon Pond Road in the north.

The state forest recommends itself as a place for a weekend campout. You have several choices: you may backpack to one of the bivouac areas (Morrell Brook in the south or Sum Gay Gulf in the north), or stay at the convenient camping area right off the main paved road, Taylor Valley Road. The FLT passes through this area, where there are picnic tables, fireplaces, and several dozen campsites. A camping permit is required here. To obtain one, call or write: Regional Wildlife Manager, P.O. Box 1169, Cortland, N.Y. 13045 (607-753-3095).

Access. The camping area at Taylor Valley Road can be reached via NY 91 out of Truxton to Cheningo; NY 91 now becomes Taylor Valley Road, and two miles from Cheningo you see the camping area on both sides of the road. Truxton can be reached from Cortland via NY 13 or from Syracuse via NY 91.

Trail. You can combine the FLT with a number of hard-surfaced dirt roads, truck trails, and lanes to form loops in both the southern and northern portions of the state forest.

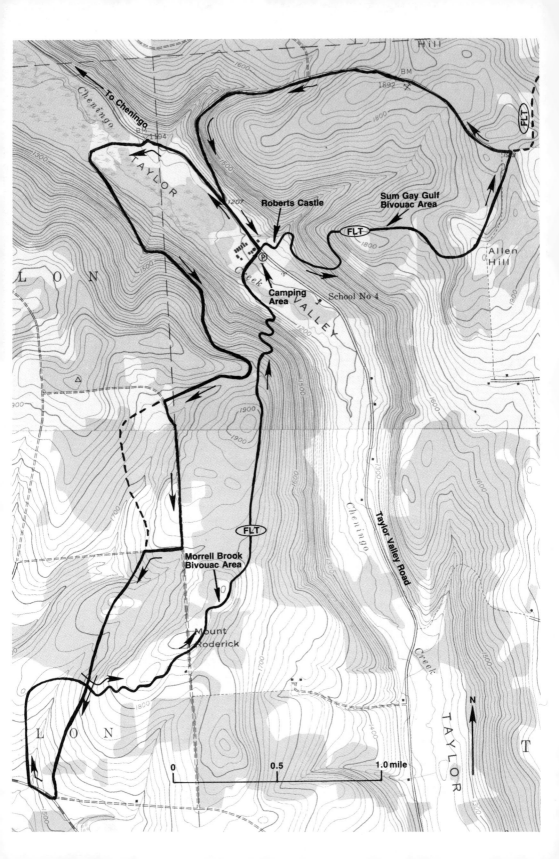

Beaver pond in Taylor Valley State Forest

First Day

*Taylor Valley Road to Telephone Road
and back
Distance: 8 miles
Hiking time: 4 hours*

We'll assume you have decided to stay at Taylor Valley Road, so try the southern loop first. Start by walking north on Taylor Valley Road from the campsite for almost a mile, where an unnamed dirt road intersects on the left. This road takes you into a small wooded area where soon the trees give way to a marshy spot through which Cheningo Creek flows. The marsh with its several small ponds and waterholes is a good place for waterfowl. If you're lucky, you may see some mallards in the water or taking off as you approach. The area also is home to quite a few large snapping turtles.

The road crosses Cheningo Creek, turns left, and heads uphill now under a canopy of trees. A mile brings you to the top of the hill for a vertical rise of 600 feet. Here the road loops to the right, and in ½ mile further comes to an intersection. Take the lane forking off on your left. The lane runs due south for almost a mile, where a road comes in from the right. Turn west onto this road, and a short walk brings you to another intersection.

Turn left here, and follow this dirt road south. It soon crosses what in the spring is a small brook, rises gradually for a while, and then starts descending until it reaches the intersection with Mount Roderick Road and Telephone Road. Turn right onto the highway (Telephone Road), and walk a short distance downhill untiil you see the white blazes on a tree on your right that indicate the beginning of the FLT.

Turn right onto the trail, which runs due north for a little over ½ mile, and then turns right and uphill. Follow the trail as it runs east. The uphill climb is steady (past a gravel pit) until you reach the summit of Mount Roderick; this area, called Aspen Ridge, is open, with some fine views to the east. In a little over ¼ mile you pass Morrell Brook bivouac area.

The terrain is now fairly level. A ½ mile more on the trail brings you back into the hardwood forest, where the trail now begins to pitch downward, with a drop so gradual you are hardly aware of it. A mile further brings you to a small hilltop pond on the western edge of the trail, which might be a nice place for lunch.

Just beyond the pond, the trail begins a steep descent, switching back and forth as it drops 600 feet in just over ¼ mile. As it nears the bottom, it begins to level out, passing a beaver pond on the right. Look closely through the trees, and you'll see the beaver dam.

The trail now crosses a log footbridge over Cheningo Creek, and in another few minutes you are back at your campsite.

Second Day

Taylor Valley Road via Allen Hill and back
Distance: 4 miles
Hiking time: 2 hours

Follow the FLT markers on the north side of Taylor Valley Road in an area called Roberts Castle. The FLT follows a lane for a short distance, and then turns sharply right to head up a steep hill.

It is a steady climb for the next mile, as the trail loops first to the right and ¼ mile later to the left. Soon the terrain levels off, and you come to an open area called the Sum Gay Gulf bivouac area. For the next ¼ mile the terrain is level, but then it begins to rise, and again you start to climb.

When you break out of the forest on the western slope of Allen Hill, a short distance more over a field brings you to the top of Allen Hill. About every three to four years, the farmer who owns the hilltop plows it and plants grain. In between, the hilltop is a hayfield. The view south from here is great.

When you leave the woods and start across the field, hold a steady course. As you reach the hill's crest, you see ahead of you on a fencepost two white blazes. Here the FLT turns left onto a lane, which it follows for about ¼ mile, when it then leaves the lane, forking to the right and up the side of a hill. It soon crosses another lane, re-enters the woods, and then comes back out on the lane again.

In less than ¼ mile on this lane you come to an intersection with another lane. You can turn right on the FLT here and head east. It is a gradual downhill walk until you near Cheningo-Solon Pond Road; the trail then makes a steeper descent to the road itself. Here you catch a nice view up and down the valley and across the valley to Cuyler Hill (see Hike 19).

If you don't want to hike to Cheningo-Solon Pond Road and retrace your steps, you can leave the FLT by turning left on the lane. A short walk west brings you to a hard-surfaced dirt road, which you follow in a westerly direction. At first the road is level, but soon it slopes downward for almost ¼ mile before heading uphill. In ¼ mile more you come to a gravel pit on the right and the height of land. The crest of Seacord Hill is off on the right.

Continue on the dirt road as it heads downhill. The vista ahead to the west is an attractive one. Soon you come to another dirt road intersecting on the right. Continue past this road on your downward trek. The descent becomes more pronounced now. Soon the road turns left and pitches down even more sharply. It is ½ mile more to Taylor Valley Road. Turn left onto the highway, and follow it back to your camping area.

18

Bucks Brook State Forest

Total distance: 8 miles
Hiking time: 4 hours
Vertical rise: 760 feet
Map: USGS 7½′ South Otselic

The charm of this place is its unpretentiousness. A tract of state land east of Cortland, it is known officially as Bucks Brook State Forest, just a forested hilltop where you can hike quietly along a section of the Finger Lakes Trail (FLT).

Yet as the poet Ezra Pound noted "Learn of the green world what can be thy place." Perhaps you will find this small hilltop such a green world, for the pleasure of walking is somehow heightened here. In spring, when the trees put on the season's first yellow-green dress, the hilltop becomes a delight of renewal. In summer, it turns into a cathedral of green coolness. In autumn, amidst the fall foliage of yellows and reds, it evokes a wistful memory of summer gone.

Here, as with some other areas along the FLT, there are problems of map names and other official designation. The state Lands and Forests Division uses a departmental name: Chenango 20. A later and less technical label given this same area by the state is Bucks Brook State Forest, after the stream running through it, although no one around here seems to use this title. The map published by the Finger Lakes Trail Conference calls the hilltop over which the FLT runs McDermott Hill, making this the popular name. However, if you are using a recent USGS quadrangle map you will find no McDermott Hill listed, nor will you find any indication that this is even state land. Finally, although most state forests have special name signs posted along the roadways through them, you will find no such signs here. To the average person passing through this forest, it is simply a quiet wooded place.

The suggested loop, which follows a completed section of the FLT out and dirt roads back, is a good day's hike. It takes you through an inviting stand of hardwoods and evergreens, over quietly flowing, sun-flecked brooks, through a small gorge, and to a hilltop from which you can see the surrounding countryside stretching away in all directions. And should you wish to spend the night, there is an ideal campsite in a partial clearing near McDermott Hill. During the day this fern swale is warmed by shafts of sunlight, and during the night it collects and holds the soft talk of the night peepers.

When you walk, do so slowly; this wooded area is host to a great number of mushrooms, and if you look carefully along the path's edges, you may see, as I did, as impressive variety on a day's walk. Watch for the various amanitas, collybias, galerinas, pholiotas, russulas, and polypores, especially *polyporus versicolor,* or "turkey tails." Bring along your mushroom field guide; it makes identification easier and more fun.

Access. This state forest lies between DeRuyter and South Otselic. From DeRuyter on NY 13, take the DeRuyter Turnpike south three miles to the top of the hill where Ridge Road (dirt) cuts off on your right. Follow Ridge Road 1.5 miles to Ratville Road, another dirt road,

where you turn right. Past the second house (and barn), Ratville Road narrows to a single lane. One mile from that point, you encounter trail markers—hand-lettered words painted on trees on both sides of the road—for the McDermott Hill section of the FLT. Park in the small area off the road just beyond.

Trail. Turn left (southeast) onto the FLT. It leads you uphill through the woods for ½ mile, and then, on more level terrain, gradually loops to the left (north). After ¼

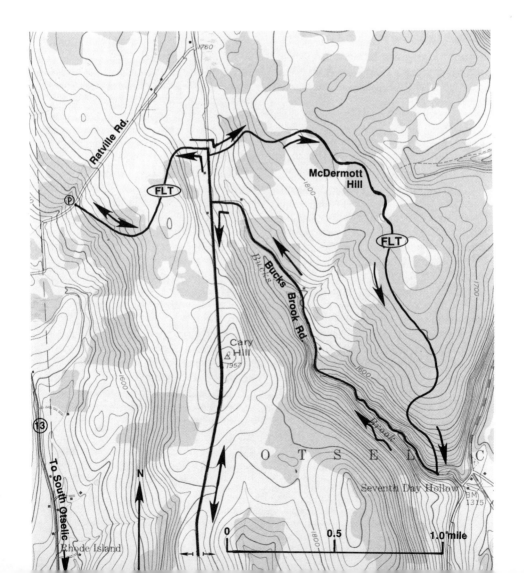

mile, it turns right (east) and a short distance beyond brings you to Ridge Road. Walk along the road to the right (south) for about 25 yards to pick up the trail on the other side. Soon after you re-enter the woods, you slant downhill and cross a small stream. This is Bucks Brook, which flows south and eventually empties into the Otselic River just below the hamlet of Seventh Day Hollow.

From here the trail moves uphill through evergreens that soon give way to maple and beech. At the crest the land flattens, indicating that you are now walking a ridge. Soon you enter a stand of tall, well-spaced red spruce, one of the several attractive areas in this forest.

The trail now swings gradually to your right and heads south. Soon it pitches downward, taking you into a small gully where in spring a brook flows eastward. In summer the gully is usually dry. The trail leads up the other side to another level. On your right is one of the area's highest points (el. 1,860 feet), designated as McDermott Hill on the FLT map.

You soon come to a partial clearing filled with ferns. If you are planning to camp overnight, this may be the place you will want to stay.

Continuing south ½ mile, you begin a gradual descent. Within the next ½ mile the slope steepens, and as you near the trail's end the downward pitch becomes quite pronounced. The FLT terminates on Bucks Brook Road (dirt) in a modest-sized gorge called Seventh Day Hollow. The gorge's vertical sides are exposed shale, and its bottom is just wide enough to accommodate the road and Buck's Brook. The creek bed and exposed sites by the roadside are good places to search for fossils.

Now turn right on Bucks Brook Road and head north. Following the twists and turns of the brook, the road ascends gradually, rising out of the gorge into a ravine and then into a wider-bottomed hollow. One mile from the trail's end, you emerge from the woods; fields spread off to your right along the lower side of McDermott Hill. You soon re-enter another wooded section from which you emerge in ¼ mile. A short climb up a small, open hill brings you to Ridge Road. If you wish to shorten your hike, you can turn right (north) now and head back toward your vehicle.

The full hike, however, continues south on Ridge Road to a fine overlook. You reach the summit of Cary Hill (el. 1,957 feet) in ¾ mile. The wooded areas on both sides prevent you from enjoying any vistas, though, so walk another mile to the ridge's next high point. Here fields on both sides of the road allow you fine views of rolling hills to the east and west.

When ready, turn around and walk back along Ridge Road, past the intersection of Bucks Brook Road and, ¼ mile beyond, to the FLT crossing. Turn left here. Another ½ mile brings you to your vehicle on Ratville Road.

This is good ski touring and snowshoeing country. The snows come often and stay on the ground long, especially in the forest. Ridge Road is plowed in winter, allowing you access to the FLT, the northern end of which is ideal for ski touring. The southern section from McDermott Hill to Bucks Brook Road is too steep to negotiate on skis.

Cuyler Hill State Forest

Total distance: 7½ miles
Hiking time: 4½ hours
Vertical rise: 1,364 feet
Maps: USGS 7½' Cuyler; FLT Map "Randall Hill"

It is not always easy to put a name to a hike. This one could be called the Randall Hill hike, as it takes you over Randall Hill, a seven-mile-long ridge northeast of Cortland. I prefer to call it Cuyler Hill, after the thickly-wooded state forest that runs almost the full length of that high but relatively level ridge. Whatever the name, this is an area that quickly can become a favorite for both day hikes and overnight backpacking.

Here you walk the well-marked Randall Hill section of the Finger Lakes Trail (FLT), which was constructed and is maintained by the Onondaga Chapter of the Adirondack Mountain Club. Running along the flattened crest of Randall Hill, making for easy-to-moderate walking, the trail meanders through tall, well-spaced hardwoods, stands of evergreens, swales of ferns, and cool glens with quietly flowing brooks. It is the central portion of a 21-mile stretch of maintained and marked trails in this part of New York state: to the south the FLT leads a little over 10 miles to Mount Roderick near Solon and to the northwest, about 11 miles to NY 26 near Otselic Center.

The 7¾-mile loop recommended here includes a short detour to a lean-to and a scenic overlook.

Access. To reach Cuyler Hill for the start of this hike, take NY 13 northeast from Cortland or south from Cazenovia to Cuyler, a hamlet of two dozen homes slightly off NY 13. In the center of the hamlet, turn east onto Lincklaen Road, and drive for two miles to Cuyler Hill Road, on the right just beyond a small house. Turn here, and drive uphill for 1.1 miles to a cluster of farm buildings where the paved road intersects a dirt one. Turn left onto the dirt road (a continuation of Cuyler Hill Road), and drive 0.4 mile to Stoney Brook Road, the first dirt road on the left. Continue uphill on this road. At 0.3 mile you reach woods and the edge of Cuyler Hill State Forest. Looking back from here, you have a wide vista of long valleys, pastureland, and wooded hilltops. Two miles to the west rises Pease Hill and further west the Morgan and Truxton hills (see Hike 11).

In another 0.2 mile, watch for the word "Hike" painted in white on a tree to your right. This is where the Randall Hill Section of the FLT crosses the road. Park your vehicle here.

Trail. Begin your walk by following the trail south, downhill into the forest. Within a few feet you come to several trail

Cuyler Hill

0   0.5   1.0 mile

FLT

P

Stoney Brook Road

1825

N
1900

1795

1800

Cuyler   Hill Road

2000

1600

1700

Elwood Road

Enz Road

Spring

1900

HILL

Randall   Hill Road

1700

1900

Randall

1900

FLT

signs—white lettering painted on a large tree on the left—that read "Cuyler Summit 1 mi," "Rose Hollow 2½ mi," and "Randall Hill Rd 3 mi." The trail markers along the main FLT are white; those on spur trails are orange.

In about ½ mile the trail passes over what in spring and early summer is Bundy Creek, although by late summer it may be a dry streambed. Another ½ mile brings you to Cuyler Summit, the high point of Randall Hill (el. 2,080 feet). Beyond it, the trail is relatively flat for a stretch before starting a gradual descent. In about ½ mile, after making a sharp left turn and then one to the right, you see an orange-marked spur trail forking to your left. This leads to Elwood Road, a dirt lane running parallel to the main trail. Continue on the main trail for another ¾ mile, through several fern swales, over another high point, called Kiwi Summit (el. 2,020 feet) on the FLT map, and finally to a second spur to Elwood Road. Shortly the main trail passes over a third high point, called Accordion Summit (el. 2,020 feet) on the FLT map.

About ¼ mile beyond, the trail forks. Here, painted on a tree, a white-lettered sign reads "Rose Hollow" with an arrow pointing right. Bearing right and following the orange-blazed spur trail downhill for ¼ mile, you come to the Rose Hollow lean-to, which overlooks a small gully cut by Enz Brook. Near the lean-to look for two signs hand-lettered on trees; one directs you to an overlook to the southwest, the other to a spring. In summer the vista from the overlook is restricted by the full-foliaged trees. Try the spring trail for some refreshing cold water and a much better view. In ⅛ mile it leads you across the brook to the small productive spring and the trail's end. If you bear left here and walk another 100 feet through the woods, you step into a field, where you have an excellent view of the distant, wooded tops of Seacord and Allen hills.

Retrace your steps to the main trail, turn right, and continue walking south. The trail now pitches gradually downhill through large stands of maples and smaller stands of evergreens to Randall Hill Road. The FLT heads across the road and into the forest, but to continue your hike, turn left and walk this road for a little under a mile, until it intersects Elwood Road. At the corner on your right you can see a clearing with makeshift fireplaces. This camping area is one of several spots, along with the lean-to, where you can stay on an overnight outing.

Turn left on Elwood Road and walk another mile to the orange markers and Hike sign that indicate the entrance to one of the spur trails you passed on your way out. Turn left here and walk the short distance (1,000 feet) back to the main trail, where you turn right (north). You are now 2½ miles south of your starting point. In less than an hour you should be back on Stoney Brook Road where you left your vehicle.

This area is ideal for ski touring and snowshoeing. The main trail has enough variation in terrain to make skiing interesting, and it is long enough to allow you to ski all day. As the roads in the state forest are not plowed in winter, they too can be used for touring. The snowfall is heavy here and the forest holds it well to the end of March, and sometimes into early April.

Cuyler Hill State Forest

20

Tuller Hill State Forest

Total distance: 9½ miles
Hiking time: 5 hours
Vertical rise: 1,330 feet
Maps: USGS 7½′ McGraw; USGS 7½′ Cortland

Nice things can come in small packages, as the Tuller Hill State Forest shows. Here are tall, spaced hardwoods and tight stands of evergreens, peaked hilltops and rounded knolls, deep ravines and gentle glens, rushing brooks and meandering streams, and, for those who like to see the rugged countryside as well as feel it, numerous overlooks. Tucked in this cluster of wooded hills south of Cortland and just west of the Tioughnioga River are abandoned roads and jeep trails and a short, relatively new trail that is a delight to hike.

The Tuller Hill Trail, constructed by the Onondaga Chapter of the Adirondack Mountain Club, eventually will be joined to other trails to form part of the state-wide Finger Lakes Trail system (FLT). This stretch has also been designated part of the North Country Trail, a route that, while still largely in the planning stage, will someday wend across the northern part of the United States from New York to North Dakota. On this hike, you follow the well-groomed and clearly-blazed (in white) Tuller Hill Trail out and a series of dirt roads and trails back.

Access. To reach the trailhead, follow NY 90 west from NY 11 in Homer (north of Cortland), passing through the hamlet of Messengerville. At four miles, watch for Carson Road, which cuts sharply back and uphill on your right. Follow this road 1.2 miles to the top of the hill, where the forest edge comes right to the road. Park here. The word "Hike" painted in white on a tree to your left marks the southern entry to the Tuller Hill section of the FLT. Before entering the woods, though, pause long enough to enjoy the excellent view south overlooking the Gridley Creek valley. The hills are tree-covered and their sides steep; the valley is narrow and winding.

Trail. From your vantage point at 1,700 feet above sea level, you climb another 200 feet over the next ¼ mile to the level summit of Tut Hill. For the next ¾ mile, the trail runs along the ridge of Tut Hill; it then starts a gradual descent into Riordan Hollow, crosses Riordan Brook, and, bearing left, continues its downward journey another ¾ mile into Woodchuck Hollow. At 1,500 feet, this hollow is the lowest point in the Tuller Hill Forest.

In the hollow, the trail turns north along an abandoned wagon road that parallels Woodchuck Brook, which flows southward through the relatively deep cut between Tut, Audubon, and Snyder Hills on the east and Woodchuck and Tuller Hills

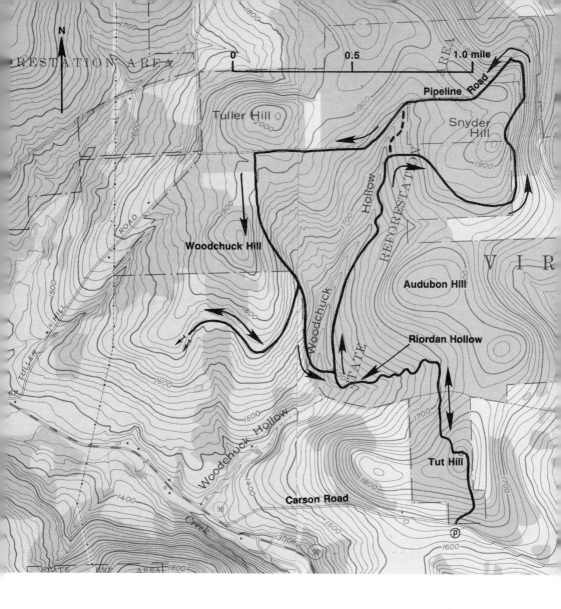

on the west. The canopy of trees, the wide lane, and the sound of running water make this section of the hike especially attractive—so much so that you scarcely notice the gradual uphill grade. In about ¾ mile, a small clearing and the Woodchuck Hollow lean-to come into view. You can camp here if you are on an overnight hike.

As it passes the lean-to, the trail leaves the old wagon road. After ½ mile, it brings you to the Neal Brook spur trail, which is blazed with orange markers. Your route, the main trail, follows the white blazes to the right and uphill.

Swinging southeast, you cross a dirt road in ¼ mile and a pipeline right-of-way in another ¼ mile. Here the trail turns north again, following the contour of Snyder Hill. Several overlooks allow you to enjoy the scenery across the Tioughnioga River to the east.

Still following the contours of Snyder Hill, the trail bends left, and you climb almost to the summit (el. 1,900 feet) before bearing right. After a moderate descent for ¼ mile, the trail intersects a dirt road unimaginatively called Pipe Line Road. In ½ mile you should spot the other entrance to the Neal Brook spur trail by the edge of a small ravine on the left. Remain on Pipe Line Road. In about ¾ mile, watch for a jeep trail leading away from the road on your left. Directly opposite, about 1,000 feet through the stand of hardwoods, you can see the summit of Tuller Hill, at 2,010 feet the highest point in the state forest. To get to its summit you have to bushwhack.

Turn left to follow the jeep trail, which is relatively level for nearly ¼ mile before it heads downhill; here, about 500 feet off to your right, is yet another high point in the forest, Woodchuck Hill. The top of this hill is forested, but the lower sections are not.

Continuing downhill for just over ¼ mile, the trail reaches the state forest's boundary. For a magnificient overlook, stay on the unmarked foot trail as it bends slightly right and flattens out to follow the contour of a hill through stands of saplings and small trees. After ¼ mile, it swings uphill and in another ¾ mile brings you to an open field, where the trail ends. Before you spreads a grand view of valleys and distant hills. Immediately below is the Gridley Creek valley, NY 90, and Virgil Creek valley; directly across are the ski slopes of Greek Peak on Virgil Mountain.

After drinking in the view, retrace your steps to the state forest boundary. If you look off to your right at the forest edge, you should spot an abandoned road running gradually downhill. (During the winter, this old road becomes a snowmobile trail.) Walk down this track nearly ½ mile to a gully on your left, and then follow this gully to the base of the hill and Woodchuck Brook. Cross the stream and climb the embankment opposite. On top you intersect the main Tuller Hill Trail you hiked earlier. Turn right and head back 1¾ miles to your vehicle.

The snow is deep here, and it lasts well into March, providing excellent ski touring and snowshoeing conditions along the main trail and Pipe Line Road.

21

Kennedy Memorial Forest

Total distance: 9 miles
Hiking time: 4 hours
Vertical rise: 1,523 feet
Map: USGS 7½′ Harford

To the hiker, the high spot in this area is called Virgil Mountain; to the downhill skier it is Greek Peak. The hiker gets to the top by foot, the skier by chairlift.

Once on top in whatever season, you have a grand view to the north, east, and southeast. To the east and southeast is a deep cleft through which Gridley Creek runs. To the north across the narrow Gridley Creek valley is Tuller Hill. Looking northwest several miles, you can see the hamlet of Virgil nestled in Virgil Creek valley.

The 4,554-acre state forest, named in memory of Jack Kennedy, the regional forester who developed this area, occupies the high terrain up to the western edge of Virgil Mountain. The hill's eastern side, with a sharp downhill drop of almost 1,000 feet, is private land owned by the Greek Peak Ski Center, which operates three chairlifts on that side of the mountain.

The highland area of the state forest is knobby, with six spots rising to elevations of over 2,000 feet. Virgil Mountain is the highest at 2,132 feet. Other high spots range from 2,010 to 2,070 feet, but the most spectacular view is from the top of Virgil Mountain. The terrain making up Kennedy Forest is also dissected by a half dozen streams that have cut narrow valleys, or hollows. The best known are Babcock Hollow in the central sector and Quail Hollow, two miles to the east.

Running through almost the entire east-west width of Kennedy Forest is the Finger Lakes Trail (FLT), a groomed and well-marked foot-trail. At this writing, a small section of trail toward the east is still being built, eventually to connect with the FLT in Tuller State Forest (see Hike 20).

Access. The trailhead can be reached most easily from Virgil, which is on NY 90 six miles south of Cortland. Once in Virgil, take the Virgil-Harford Road (County Route 128) south for two miles to its intersection with Babcock Hollow Road. Turn left (east) onto Babcock Hollow Road, which takes you east for a while and then south. From the intersection, drive 2.4 miles, where you will see a sign indicating the beginning of the state forest. White blazes on trees on both sides of the road also indicate where the FLT crosses the road. The FLT is just a short distance south of a mobile home on the right side of the road. This is the trailhead, so park here.

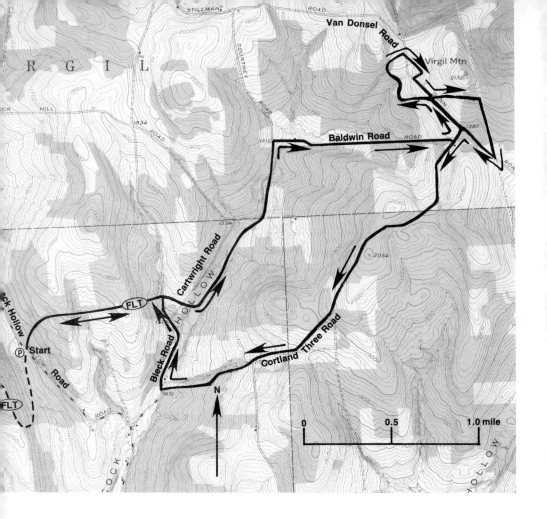

Trail. This hike uses the FLT as well as some of the dirt roads in the forest, allowing you to walk a loop. Starting at Babcock Hollow Road, you begin your hike on the FLT with an uphill climb of over ¼ mile; the vertical rise is 300 feet. The trail then makes a sharp descent, crosses a brook, and climbs another hill following the south edge of the woods. Here you have a fine view to the south.

Another ¼ mile brings you to the hill's top, and the trail now starts another sharp descent, dropping 230 feet into a narrow, wooded valley where it crosses another small creek. A short climb uphill brings you to Bleck Road; cross the road, and continue on the FLT as it re-enters the woods. A short distance beyond, the trail crosses a dirt road (Cartright Road) and descends a steep bank to a creek, where it turns to follow the creek northward.

In little over ½ mile, the trail intersects and follows an old road uphill; you will notice several old building foundations nearby, probably remains of farmhouse and barn. A little beyond, the trail leaves

Looking west from Virgil Mountain in Kennedy Memorial Forest

the old road to follow a logging road north. In slightly less than ½ mile, the trail leaves the woods and intersects a dirt road (Cartright Road again), which the trail now follows north to the intersection with Baldwin Road. The FLT continues northward on the dirt road for a little over ¼ mile before ending.

You, however, turn right onto Baldwin Road and hike due east. The road passes open fields and a house on the left, crosses two small creeks, and starts a gradual ascent. From the last intersection, it is a mile hike to the next intersection.

When you reach the intersection, turn left onto Cortland Three Road. A short walk brings you to the intersection with Van Donsel Road. Turn left, and follow the relatively level road northward for a little over ¼ mile. Here part of the (white-blazed) FLT crosses the road. Turn left (west) onto the FLT; it takes you on a loop, across a gully, and uphill where it crosses Van Donsel Road again. Stay on the trail as it re-enters the woods. After a short uphill climb, you come to the edge of a clearing. You have reached the top of Virgil Mountain, and ahead and to your left you can see the Greek Peak summit station.

The marked trail, however, remains in the woods, turns right, and heads downhill along the edge of a ski trail. A short distance downhill, it intersects with an abandoned road. Turn right onto this road, and a short walk westward brings you back onto Van Donsel Road. Turn left to retrace your steps southward on Van Donsel Road until you again intersect the FLT you took earlier. This time, however, turn east (left) onto the trail, and follow it uphill for ¼ mile. It ends at an intersection with a one-lane service road running under powerlines. Here you have a fine view to the east.

Turn right onto the service road, and follow it south for ½ mile to where it intersects with Van Donsel Road. Turn right, and follow Van Donsel Road northward for a little over ¼ mile to the intersecttion with Cortland Three Road. Stay on Cortland Three Road as it runs southward. You start a gradual climb, and in slightly over ½ mile you reach the top of the hill with the road leveling out at an elevation of 2,054 feet.

From here your course is downhill for the next 1½ miles; en route there are some nice views to the west. Several lanes and dirt roads intersect on the left, but you continue on Cortland Three Road until it runs into Black Road. At this intersection, turn right and follow the road northward past Cartright Road for a little over ½ mile until the FLT that you walked earlier crosses the road. Turn left, and you can now retrace your steps on the FLT to your starting point.

22

Hammond Hill State Forest

Total distance: 5 miles
Hiking time: 2½ hours
Vertical rise: 584 feet
Map: USGS 7½' Dryden

As you drive south from Cortland to the village of Dryden, you'll see highlands ahead, stretching along an east-west axis and standing like a huge wall. These hills rise to almost 1,000 feet from the flatlands in the north to form a hilly plateau that pitches gradually down toward the south.

On top of the highlands, you'll find a wide valley formed by low hills—a most attractive landscape in any season, but most scenic in spring and summer. The few farms left on the hill use this land mostly for pasture.

As in other hilltop areas, the land's low fertility here makes for poor crop farming. Farmers discovered that after the turn of the century and gradually left farming for other occupations, an exodus accelerated by the Great Depression. It was during the 1930s and 1940s that the state acquired tracts of land in this region. Today they are identified as Yellow Barn State Forest, Robinson Hollow State Forest, and Hammond Hill State Forest. All are close neighbors, virtually touching one another as you travel south.

Occupying the central region is the largest of the three, the 3,545-acre Hammond Hill State Forest. It features several high spots. Near the forest's northern

boundary is Star Stanton Hill, with two knobs rising to elevations of 2,008 and 2,011 feet. About a half mile to the south is Hammond Hill itself, with an elevation of 1,970 feet.

The state forest has no marked or groomed trails; there are, however, several single-lane dirt roads and some abandoned wagon roads (now just narrow lanes) that serve well as hiking trails. Two dirt roads run through the forest. Hammond Hill Road, the main access road, runs in an east-west direction through the northern sector. Canaan Road, which intersects Hammond Hill Road in the middle of the forest, runs south along the headwaters of Owego Creek, eventually intersecting Canaan Valley Road 2¾ miles to the south.

Access. To reach Hammond Hill State Forest, take NY 13 9.5 miles south from Cortland to Dryden, or NY 13 northeast from Ithaca for 14 miles to Dryden. Once in Dryden, drive west 0.5 miles on NY 13 from the signal light in the center of the village to Irish Settlement Road, intersecting on the south. Turn here and head south uphill, continuing over the ridge for 3.5 miles to Hammond Hill Road on the left. Turn east onto this dirt road, and drive ½ mile to the intersection with Canaan Road. Park here.

Trail. On the north side of the road, you will see a small clearing in the woods and the start of a truck road; on the left of this road is a little-used lane, heading in a northwesterly direction. Follow this trail as it continues westward uphill for ¼ mile. It now turns right (north) and runs on level ground for another ¼ mile to where it turns right (east).

After a relatively short uphill climb, you reach the top of the western knob of Star Stanton Hill; another ¼ mile takes you through a slight depression and then up to the hill's second knob. The trail now turns right (south) and heads downhill through a mixed stand of evergreen and hardwood for ¼ mile, where you intersect Hammond Hill Road. Turn right (west) on this road, and head uphill; the climb is a modest one, and in less than ¼ mile you are back at the intersection with Canaan Road.

Turn south onto Canaan Road. Forking to the left here is a narrow, little-used lane; to the right is the wider Canaan Road, on which you stay. A little over ¼ mile brings you to the high point of the road, the crest of Hammond Hill. Ahead of you is a fine view of the hills to the south.

The road now begins to descend, and for the next mile it is all downhill until you see a road intersecting on the left at a point where Canaan Road levels out and approaches the narrow Owego Creek.

Turn left onto this unnamed road. The first ¼ mile is fairly level, but then the

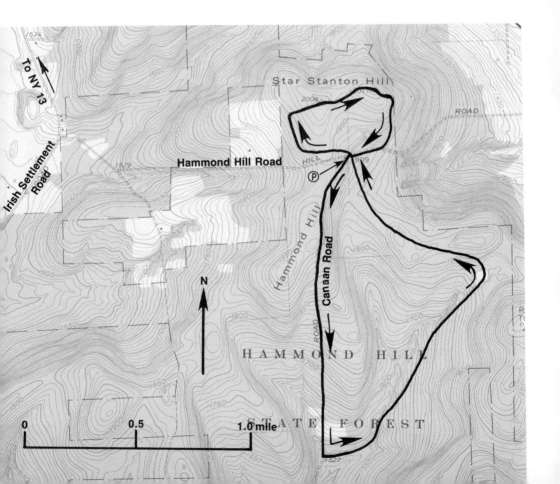

View looking south from top of Hammond Hill

road crosses a branch of Owego Creek and starts uphill, where the going is relatively steep. At the mile mark, the road on which you have been hiking ends, giving way to a fairly large open area—a landing, loading, and turn-around point for lumber trucks. At the end of the road and somewhat to the left, you'll see a foot-trail that climbs a small hill and levels out.

Follow the foot-trail as it heads north for a short distance and then turns sharply west. For the next ½ mile, the easy hiking is on level ground, but then the trail starts a modest climb on what now becomes a narrow lane. In less than ¼ mile you will be back at the intersection of Hammond Hill Road and Canaan Road where you left your vehicle.

Lincklaen State Forest

Total distance: 10 miles
Hiking time: 5 hours
Vertical rise: 1,040 feet
Maps: USGS 7½′ South Otselic; USGS 7½′ Pitcher

The name Lincklaen has a nice highland ring to it; and the name fits the region, with its diverse terrain, peaked tree-covered hilltops, and narrow wedge-shaped valleys that provide a fine scenic environment in the Susquehanna Hill Region.

Lincklaen State Forest is located between DeRuyter to the north and South Otselic to the south. The 4,514-acre state forest looks something like a checkerboard, with small parcels of private land scattered throughout the state land. It is roughly rectangular in shape, about three miles wide and six miles long.

The nearest civilization to the trailhead is South Otselic, about two miles south of the forest's southern boundary on NY 26. About 1½ miles north of the northern boundary is the hamlet of Lincklaen Center, nestled in a narrow valley.

Several high places in the region afford the hiker some excellent vistas. Lane Hill (el. 1,860 feet) dominates the forest's west-central sector, and, despite its name, South Hill (el. 1,800 feet) is located on the northern edge of the state forest. Five other unnamed high spots, generally within the 1,800 foot range, are found in and around the state forest, to give a good account of the area's hilliness.

Lincklaen State Forest is a little off the beaten path, which is what gives it some added appeal. Several miles to the north is Mariposa State Forest; a little to the east is Bucks Brook State Forest (see Hike 18); and the Finger Lakes Trail that passes through both of them makes them a popular target for hikers and backpackers. Lincklaen, in contrast, goes virtually unnoticed as hiking country, so when you get there you may have it to yourself.

Access. The easiest access to the trailhead is from NY 26 in the village of South Otselic. South Otselic, in turn, can be reached from Cortland (and I-81) on the west via NY 41, or from Syracuse and Cazenovia in the north via NY 13 and NY 80. Once in South Otselic, drive southwest on NY 26 for 2.5 miles, and turn right (north) onto Kemak Road (a dirt road). Drive north on Kemak Road for 1.4 miles to an intersection. Park here.

Trail. The state forest does not have any marked hiking trails. You hike on truck trails and lanes. From your parking spot, start your hike on the road forking to the right. Both legs of the fork pass through narrow, scenic valleys bordering a two-mile-long ridge, which eventually peaks

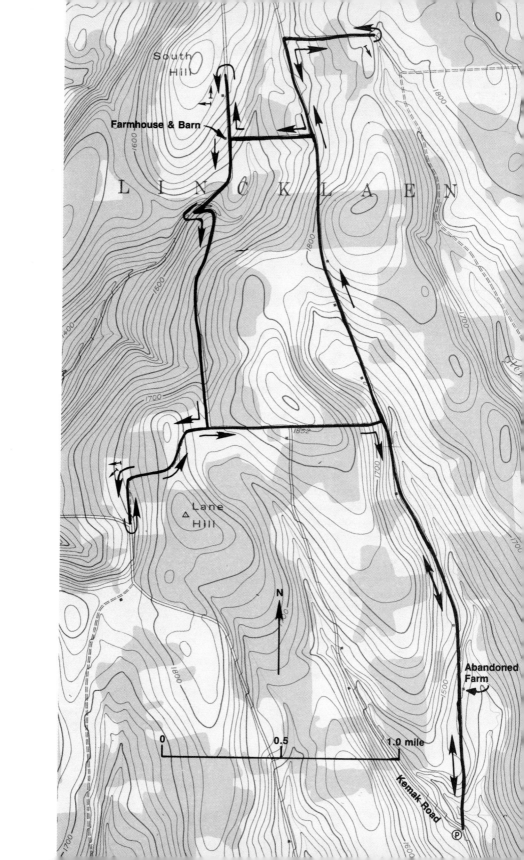

South
Hill

Farmhouse & Barn

L   I   N   C   K   L   A   E   N

Lane
△ Hill

N

Abandoned
Farm

0   0.5   1.0 mile

Kemak Road

Ⓟ

at 1,900 feet in the north. The area at the fork is open, permitting you to see quite a distance up the right-hand valley.

For the first mile, there is state land only on the left of the road; the east side, where the middle branch of Glen Brook meanders, is private land. On both sides you find hayfields that run about halfway up the hillsides on either side of the brook to forested hilltops. About ½ mile up the road, you come upon the collapsing remains of an abondoned farm. The barn and the unused house are still standing, but the out-buildings are leaning and coming apart. While the private land here is used primarily for haying, there are no longer any farms in this valley.

Continue north from here for 1¼ miles, where a lane intersects on the left and runs uphill; this is the route by which you will return. For now, stay on the main road, and another mile brings you to the crest of the hill. As you start your descent, you have an excellent view of the scenic landscape to the north and west.

On your left, the state land ends and an open field begins; state land continues for a short distance on your right. In front of you is farmland, where a small pond graces a woodlot, and a little left of the woodlot is a farmhouse and a new red barn.

Continue north downhill ½ mille to a dirt road intersecting on the left (you'll take it later). Go past this road for almost ½ mile, where another dirt road intersects on the right. Turn here, and a gradual uphill climb for almost ½ mile

brings you to the top for a long distance view to the southeast. This also may be a nice spot for a lunch break.

Retrace your steps to the last intersection. Turn left, and walk south a little over ¼ mile to a road intersecting on the right. Turn here, and ¼ mile brings you to the north-south road. Turn right here, go past the farmhouse on your left, and hike another ¼ mile to the top of the road. On your left is the knob of South Hill with a fine view to the west. Retrace your steps past the farmhouse and intersection. Continue ¼ mile downhill to a road intersecting on the left. Take this road, and follow it as it turns uphill and back into the woods. A mile further brings you to the top of Lane Hill and an east-west road.

Turn right, and follow this road as it heads downhill. In ½ mile more you come to the forest edge, where a road intersects from the right. The land here pitches downhill on the right into a narrow valley with a fine view to the west. Retrace your steps to Lane Hill and the intersection, and now continue past the intersection on a due east course for a little over ¼ mile. At this point, the road turns 90 degrees to the south. Running straight ahead, however, is a lane.

Take this lane. It runs uphill a short distance before leveling off and starting its descent. The lane runs a little over ¼ mile and then ends at the road you hiked earlier. Turn right (south), and follow the dirt road for 1½ miles back to your vehicle.

Ontario Drumlins and Hills

Chimney Bluff

Chimney Bluffs/East Bay Marsh

Total distance : 2½ miles
Hiking time: 1½ hours
Vertical rise: 150 feet
Map: USGS 7½' Sodus Point

Here's a place that delights the eye with the natural wonder of bluff sculpturing—the breathtaking sights of the "chimneys." Here you can hike a Lake Ontario beach and the edge of a 150-foot-high bluff. You also can engage in a host of enjoyable activities: a picnic on the beach, a swim in the lake, a canoe trip in the large bay and its four feeder streams, or a hike around the point.

The state owns a fair size piece of land here, made up of Chimney Bluffs Park (managed by the state's Office of Parks, Recreation, and Historic Preservation) and the East Bay Marsh Unit (managed by the state's Department of Environmental Conservation). The East Bay Marsh Unit is one of the five nearby wetland units which collectively make up the state's Lake Shore Marshes Wildlife Management Area. The park land and the East Bay Marsh Unit lie next to each other, with the former touching Lake Ontario and the latter encompassing Mudge Creek and the several other streamlets feeding into East Bay.

Initially the park land was destined to include picnic areas, park buildings, and other conventional park conveniences. Later, however, it was decided to leave the land undeveloped, and so it is today.

Access. Chimney Bluffs and East Bay Marsh areas lie 8½ miles north of the village of Clyde and a short distance east of Sodus Bay. You can reach these two areas from either Rochester in the west or Oswego in the east by taking NY 104 to where it is intersected by NY 414 which runs north from Clyde; NY 414 ends at the intersection, but the route continues north via Lake Bluff Road. Stay on this latter road for 2.8 miles where it is intersected by Lummisville Road. Turn right (east) on Lummisville Road and drive 0.9 mile to the intersection with East Bay Road. Turn left (north) on the latter road and continue north; an additional 2 miles brings you to a fork.

Take the right leg and drive 0.6 mile to where an abandoned farm road intersects on the left. Park here. (If you continue an additional 0.4 mile, you come to the edge of the Lake Ontario shore and a parking area. Several footpaths on the west side of the parking area run up the steep side of Chimney Bluffs. When these paths are wet, the hill climb can be hazardous. It is better to take the route recommended here.)

Trail. Follow the abandoned dirt road

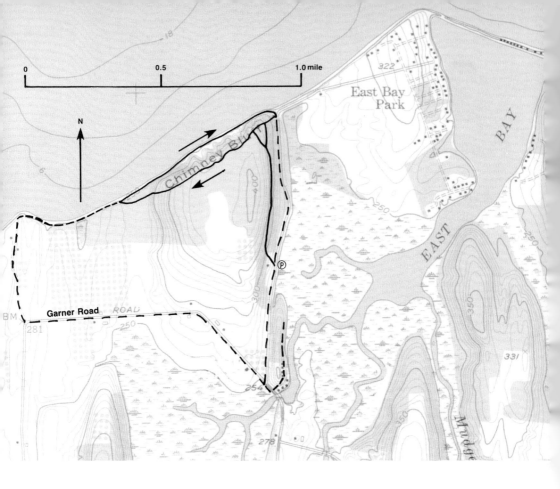

uphill from the spot where you parked your vehicle. As you get near the top of the hill, the road divides. Either leg brings you quickly to the top. In either case follow the worn footpath for several hundred yards to the edge of the eastern bluff. Here you get your first view of the "chimneys"—pinnacles, spires, peaks, saddles, and knifelike ledges that rise 150 feet above the lake edge.

These landforms have been etched, eroded, molded, and shaped by constant exposure to the winter wind, rain, icy spray, and wet snow that sweeps across Lake Ontario.

The three adjoining bluffs, each a mixture of relatively hard and soft soils,

form the face of a large drumlin—the northern half has been eaten away. This drumlin, like the hundreds of others found between Syracuse and Rochester, was formed more than 12,000 years ago when the last continental ice sheet, called the Wisconsin glacier, overran New York state. When the glacier melted back, it left a land covered with glacier-produced elongate hills or drumlins.

From Sodus Bay to within a few miles of Oswego is the Lake Ontario bluffs region; all these bluffs are drumlins that have been cut back by weathering and erosion. Such action removes the softer and more soluble soil, leaving behind the more compacted strata. Most of the bluffs are fairly flat faced. Chimney Bluffs, with their unusual shaped landforms, are the exception.

Having reached the rim of the eastern-most bluff, turn left (west) onto a footpath and follow it along the bluff edge. With every step you take the bluff scenery changes dramatically. The contrast of the red-brown pinnacles with the blue-green waters of Lake Ontario is breath-taking, especially on clear, sunny days.

Be sure to stop from time to time and drink deeply of all this. In the midst of this grandeur, don't neglect the simpler beauties that crowd around your feet. Take time, especially in late spring to observe the wildflowers that fill the woods crowning Chimney Bluffs. Sprinkled throughout are spring beauties, trout lilies, wood sorrel, buttercups, coltsfoots, may apples, foamflowers, and violets. Most striking, however, is the profusion of trilliums, Solomon's seals, and columbines.

In spring columbines are found on both sides of the path for nearly the entire distance; so, too, are the many ferns—sensitive fern, Christmas fern, and a variety of wood ferns.

Continue your walk along the rim of the eastern bluff to where a narrow finger of land extends outward; standing on this extension gives you another view of the eastern bluff to the right and also of the middle bluff. Follow the path around the edge of the middle bluff to another outward extension which separates the middle from the western bluff.

Continue on the rim path around the western bluff. Once you reach the bluff's far side, the land and path slope downward. Several hundred yards downhill

brings you to the lake's shore. Turn right (east) at this point and continue your walk on the pebble-packed shore which is 20 to 30 feet wide between the water's edge and the bluff faces.

As the chimneys come into view on your right, you have a new perspective. Looking up from down below, the bluffs take on the appearance of a strange, alien land.

Soon you reach the eastern edge of the last bluff; turn right here and climb the bank to the road and parking area. Follow the road south for 0.4 mile to your parked vehicle.

At this point, you can call it a day or continue your exploratory hike. If you are in a hiking mood, head south on the paved road (the one by which you entered), to the bridge you crossed previously. As you come to the bridge, you are overlooking a vast marsh area—a breeding ground for many of the wetland-loving birds, especially ducks. You can see the ducks moving about the marsh almost any time of day, particularly in late spring.

The marsh also makes for fine canoeing. A thin land barrier separates East Bay from Lake Ontario, and four marsh-draining streams feed the naturally impounded bay. If you wish, you can spend a day canoeing these waters. Indeed, it may take you all day, since you will cover more than ten miles of water as you canoe up and back each of the four feeder streams.

When either you or the offerings of East Bay are exhausted, retrace your steps to the beach edge and your vehicle.

Scotts Bluff/Red Creek Marsh

Total distance: 3 miles
Hiking time: 2 hours
Vertical rise: 240 feet
Map: USGS 7½′ North Wolcott

The Red Creek Marsh Unit, a state-owned parcel of wetlands and woods fronting on Lake Ontario north of Clyde and Seneca Falls, encompasses a variety of natural wonders within its two square miles. Among them are Scotts Bluff and the naturally-impounded Red Creek. The creek is ideal for flatwater canoeing and, if you like, even canoe camping along its upper reaches. The different habitats the tract encloses allow you to observe an array of both woodland and shore birds; so, beginner or expert, bring your field guide—you will find many opportunities to use it during two hours or so of easy walking around this loop. The marsh unit with its several bluffs is one of five such units which together make up the State's Lake Shores Marsh Wildlife Management Area.

The Scotts Bluff, like the other bluffs along this part of Lake Ontario, is a drumlin, a glacier-produced landform, which over thousands of years has been weathered into its present shape by the winds, rains, and storms sweeping inland from Lake Ontario.

Access. Your walk begins by Scotts Bluff, 7.6 road miles from Wolcott, which is 25 miles north of I-90 exit 41 off NY

89. Drive east out of Wolcott, toward NY 104, en route to the town of Red Creek. At 2.6 miles you cross Wadsworth Road. Another 0.8 mile brings you to Hapeman Road, where you turn left and travel 2 miles to an intersection. Turn right, drive 0.2 mile into the hamlet of North Wolcott, and turn left onto Broadway. In 0.6 mile you cross Younglove Road, 1,000 feet beyond which is a sign marking the boundary of the Red Creek Marsh Unit.

Another 0.5 mile brings you to a bridge across Red Creek, which on weekends is often lined with fishermen. All around you are wetlands where waterfowl nest, feed, and rest from early spring until late fall. About 0.9 mile beyond the bridge, the road, which turns to dirt after 0.4 mile, comes to a dead end. You are now on top of Scotts Bluff. Park your vehicle in the small parking area on the west side of the road.

Trail. At the road's end, a footpath bending slightly to the right leads to the edge of Scotts Bluff. Here, one hundred feet above the water, by a process similar to the one that produced the edges, pinnacles, peaks, and "chimneys" of Chimney Bluff (see Hike 24), winds, rains, and spray driven across Lake Ontario and

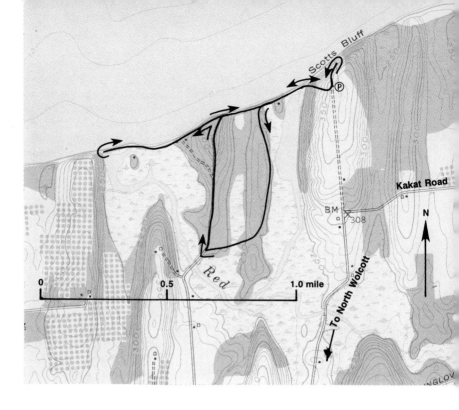

against the relatively soft earth of the cliff face have etched their marks in the form of peaks and saddles to produce this unusual landform.

Return to your vehicle. Facing west you overlook a hayfield that slopes down toward the marsh in the southwest and toward Lake Ontario in the northwest. Walk downhill to the steep trail that descends to the beach. Here an endless assortment of brightly colored pebbles and flat rocks cobbles the lakeshore. Most of the stones are of a bright reddish hue, with appealing designs on their smooth, worn surfaces. You may be tempted to fill your pockets with the most attractive ones—until you remember that you still have a mile to walk.

Back from the water's edge, tall, stately willows line the beach for ½ mile west to the next bluff. Amidst the willows, sand and dirt combine to form a natural path parallel to the lakeshore. Here, just south of the willow trees, you see what looks like a pond about ½ mile in length and 500 feet across. This is the east leg of naturally-impounded Red Creek. When heavy waves sweep across Lake Ontario during storms, they roll up tons of rocks, stones, and pebbles to form a breakwater several feet high. This breakwater then acts as a dam, preventing the water in Red Creek from emptying into the lake.

Walk west along the natural path for ¼ mile until a jeep trail angles off to the left. Follow this trail through a wooded area along the edge of the marsh. You are now heading south on a fingerlike spit of land. In ½ mile, the trail turns to your right, heading over some high ground and then through a small stretch of marsh. In just over 100 yards you come to a dirt road. Turn right and walk north, back toward Lake Ontario. This is a most pleasant place to pass through, particularly on a sunny morning when the birds are most active. The road is completely canopied by trees, mostly white oaks and maples, and there is always a cool breeze coming off the lake. Cedar waxwings, vireos, scarlet tanagers, and towhees are among the many species you migh see or hear. Spring through autumn, this wood is a noisy place, filled with the calls and songs of the feathered inhabitants.

Another ½ mile brings you to the road's end, at the edge of a 90-foot bluff, where you have an excellent view of the shoreline. To the left a footpath leads for several hundred feet into a wooded area, skirting a small clearing often used by campers. Then it bends right toward the bluff edge and slopes down to the beach, passing two summer cottages that occupy a small tract of private land.

Once on the beach, continue westward another ¼ mile. Again you find willows lining the upper shore. To the left, a narrow neck of water, part of the west leg of Red Creek, comes almost to the beach. Here you can see the interaction of water, land, wind, and waves changing the landscape almost before your eyes: one day the water may be held back by the piled-up pebbles; the next the waves may have washed some of them away, allowing the impounded waters of Red Creek to spill through the small breach into the lake.

Retrace your steps along the beach, up the path, and back to the road at the dead-end turnaround on the 90-foot-high bluff. Cross the road and walk down the field between the bluff edge and the wooded area on your right. Near the bottom a path leads through a stand of trees and back to the beach. Continue walking east for about 1,000 feet, until you see, on your right, the jeep trail you walked earlier. Take the path under the willows to the base of the bluff, and go up the footpath to your vehicle.

Howland Island Wildlife Management Area

Total distance: 4 miles
Hiking time: 2½ hours
Vertical rise: 440 feet
Map: 7½' Montezuma

The state-owned Howland Island Wildlife Management Area performs a function similar to that of its close neighbor, the Montezuma National Wildlife Refuge (Hike 27)—namely, to provide a suitable habitat for waterfowl to rest, feed, and nest. Like Montezuma, Howland attracts several hundred species of birds, including a variety of wading and shore birds. During migratory periods, Canada geese and ducks are the most numerous visitors, flying into the preserve by the hundreds.

However, there are several differences between the two refuges, some of them important to the hiker. For one, this 3,600-acre preserve is truly an island. The Seneca River flows in a huge semi-circle around its northern side, while the southern edge is bounded by the New York State Barge Canal, which, after the turn of the century, replaced the old Erie Canal. Because the Seneca River and Barge Canal merge into one another, they form an island where normally you wouldn't expect to find one.

Unlike Montezuma, most of Howland Island is best described as "upland" (fields separated by large stands of hardwood), although it is surrounded by a strip of marsh wetland along the river

and the canal. The upland section is not heavily forested; in fact there are several fields planted with corn to provide food for wildlife, particularly for geese and ducks. Interestingly, the ponds used by the waterfowl are in this upland portion, not along the lowland rim. There are also hills on the island—small ones, to be sure, but hills nonetheless. Actually, they are a cluster of glacier produced drumlins. They add variety to the landscape and provide hikers with some fine overlooks.

Still another difference is Howland's large number of ponds—11 in all. These are man-made impoundments, most of them interconnected. It is primarily in and around the ponds that a variety of management techniques are employed by the state's Department of Environmental Conservation (DEC) to provide food, cover, and shelter for over 460 species of wildlife.

This is a place to bring your bird guide and field glasses, as well as your camera. Try hiking the island during early or late spring when both land birds and waterfowl are migrating. You may see several species of hawks, including the sharp-shinned, Cooper's, red-tailed, red-shouldered, broad-winged, rough-legged, and marsh hawk. The island is laced with a network of maintenance roads that is closed to outside vehicles, so you can reach any part of the island on foot conveniently.

There are some periods when hikers are not welcome here; during the waterfowl nesting season in April and May, the entire refuge except the first mile of main road is closed to the public, and during the October and November hunting season, controlled hunting hours prevail. They are usually imposed on Tuesdays, Thursdays, and Saturdays from early morning to noon. For more specific information, call the regional DEC office in Cortland (607-753-3095).

Access. Howland Island is about eight miles northwest of Cayuga Lake and about five miles north of the New York Thruway (I-90). If you come via the Thruway, use exit 40 at Weedsport to pick up NY 31. Drive west on NY 31 to Port Byron and then north on NY 38 for two miles to Yellow Schoolhouse Road (0.5 mile beyond a set of railroad tracks). Follow this road to the left. At 1.8 miles, you cross a one-lane steel bridge over the canal. On the far side, to your right, is a public boat launching site, used extensively by fishermen and canoeists.

You are now on Howland Island. Continue on the two-lane dirt road for 0.9 mile past a dirt road intersecting on your right to a large parking area marked off by a line of large, round boulders. Park here. At the north end of the parking area where the road continues is a gate that serves as a barrier to unauthorized vehicles.

Trail. You get underway by going either of two ways. At the south end of the parking area is a footpath (on the right side) running north; in about 100 yards the path takes you past a pond on your right to a single-land dirt road also running north. The second way is to walk around the barrier gate and follow the road for 100 yards where a single-lane dirt road intersects on your right. Turn here and follow this road east for an additional 75 yards where the footpath described above intersects on your right; the road now turns north. This is your hiking route.

The road is tree-lined. On your left is a small elongated, tree-covered hill—one of more than a dozen drumlins found on

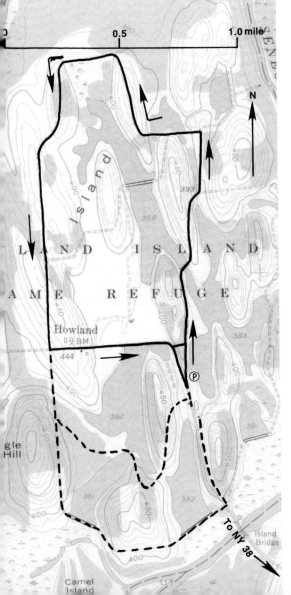

the island. As you walk northward you are actually travelling along a peninsula formed by the drumlin and the ponds on either side. Before you reach the end of the peninsula in about a mile from your starting point, the road bends slightly to the right to cross a causeway to another peninsula. Here the road makes a gradual but short ascent before pitching downward to cross a brook.

Beyond this brook, another road bears off on your right. Ignore it by keeping left past another wood-covered drumlin. About ¼ mile further on you come to a T-junction.

Here you are on high ground. Ahead, looking northeast, you can see still another pond, where, as elsewhere in the preserve, you may spot a family of geese during the summer. Turn left at the junction and head downhill (west); this brings you to more water, with the road passing over a causeway at the southern end of the pond.

You now turn north and walk over a small hill to a lowland stretch. In a short distance you may notice some swampland through the trees on your left. Soon the road starts up a gradual rise, passing a right-branching lane as it begins its loop south. You are now walking through a relatively thickly-wooded area where trees canopy the road.

Shortly the trees give way to fields on both sides. This is high ground where only small patches of trees obstruct the view. The road bends slightly to the right and then to the left, setting you on a straight southerly course; 1¼ miles more bring you to a cluster of buildings, the Howland Island staff headquarters, and another east-west road.

Turn left here. This road now runs gradually downhill for ¼ mile and then crosses another impoundment. Beyond the causeway, the road turns right (south) and in a little over ¼ mile returns you to your vehicle.

One of the other pleasant trails you can follow on the island takes you south past the staff headquarters to a fork. If you bear left, you pass through a heavily-wooded area, cross a narrow neck of another impoundment, and eventually return to your vehicle.

To lengthen your walk a bit, you can bear right at the fork and continue south past Eagle Hill on your right, across a dam, along the southern edge of still another impoundment, uphill to the main road, and then left along the road back to your vehicle. For a good view of the island, climb the short distance to the top of Eagle Hill, the highest point on the island at 570 feet.

Howland is a fine place for snowshoeing and ideal for ski touring. The terrain, with its small rolling hills, provides a whole series of short downhill runs to add a bit of excitement. Yellow Schoolhouse Road is plowed in winter, but you should check with the DEC before attempting the section leading onto the island. The snow conditions on the island are generally good, and in January and February, the snow is plentiful.

27

Montezuma National Wildlife Refuge

Total distance: 8 miles
Hiking time: 4 hours
Vertical rise: 110 feet
Maps: USGS 7½' Cayuga; USGS 7½' Savannah;
   USGS 7½' Seneca Falls

It is only a pinpoint on most maps, but each fall and spring it is a stopover for hundreds of thousands of Canada geese and an even larger number of ducks and shore birds of every variety. At the height of the migration periods, Montezuma National Wildlife Refuge draws in waterfowl the way a large magnet pulls in metal filings. In late afternoon, you can watch long skeins of geese flying into the refuge from every point of the compass. It is an impressive sight.

The 6,433-acre refuge is located at the north end of Cayuga Lake in the heart of the Finger Lakes Region. A wildlife habitat of open marsh, swamp woodland, and small sections of upland woods and fields, it is home—or at least a way station—for an impressive number of birds, mammals, and fish.

At last report, 235 species of birds and 48 species of mammals had been identified in the refuge. The latter category includes everything from the pygmy shrew to the white-tailed deer. Along with such common animals as the opossum, woodchuck, snowshoe rabbit, raccoon, fox, porcupine, beaver, and muskrat, there have been reported sightings of the southern bog lemming, mink, coyote, and even the bobcat. There are several fishing sites on the refuge where you may try your luck with brown bullheads, northern pike, walleye pike, and the hard-to-catch carp.

This is a place for binoculars, camera, and field guide. Two observation towers overlook the marshes and ponds, providing excellent opportunities for viewing the birds. There are also more than nine miles of dike roads running next to the holding pools, affording the camera buff spots for close-up shots.

Eagle "hacking" also has taken place in the refuge. Hacking refers to the hand-rearing of young eagles by man. When the eagles become self-sufficient feeders and fliers, they are banded and released by the wildlife biologists. Ten young eagles have been hacked and released since the program was introduced in 1976 by the state Department of Environmental Conservation in cooperation with the U.S. Fish and Wildlife Service and Cornell University. The hacking program has been moved to state land further west. What used to be the hacking tree or tower is located at the northern end of Tschache Pool and can be seen from the observation tower at the pool's southern end or from the Clark Ridge Overlook on the west side.

The mature eagles do return to refuge, and, if you are lucky, you may spot several flying about or sitting in trees.

Access. This waterfowl mecca is located about 20 miles west of Syracuse and 14 miles east of Geneva. It can be reached easily from US 20/NY 5, which passes south of the refuge. A sign points to the refuge entrance on the north side of the highway just west of the Cayuga-Seneca Canal and the junction with NY 90.

The entrance road takes you to a Visitor Center. Stop here to pick up maps and pamphlets. (You can also obtain these before your visit by writing: Manager, Montezuma National Wildlife Ref-

uge, RD 1, Box 232, Seneca Falls, NY 13148). Just north of the Visitor Center and past the refuge headquarters on the left of the road is an observation tower that gives you a good view of the Main Pool.

Trail. The refuge offers several excellent hiking trails: two are fairly long, and four are shorter. The problem is what to select. Not all the trails are connected footpaths, so the starting points of several are best reached by vehicle.

The three routes recommended here are the May's Point Pool trail ("M"), the Tschache Pool trail ("T"), and the Esker

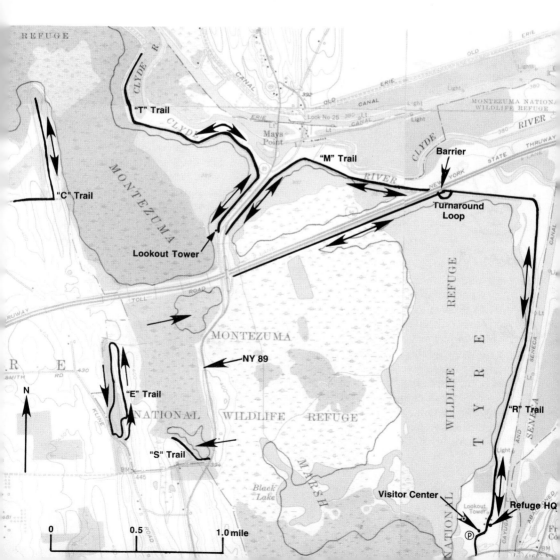

Brook Trail ("E").

From the Visitor Center, a two-lane dirt road (the "R" trail) runs north along the eastern edge of the Main Pool for 2 miles where it turns west. An additional 0.5 mile on this western portion of the road brings you to a road barrier and a turn-around spot. The sign on the barrier informs you that no unauthorized vehicles are allowed to continue westward; however, if you wish, you can walk along this road for 1.25 miles where you intersect a two-lane blacktop road, NY 89, running north and south.

With the "R" trail you have several choices; you can walk it, bike it, or drive it. The road gives you a fine view of the Main Pool where you can observe resting, feeding, or flying waterfowl. Half way down the road the pool's outlet feeds into the near-by Cayuga-Seneca Canal. Large carp cluster here during the spring spawning season.

To get to the "T" and "M" trails, return to the Visitor Center and drive out the way you came in to US 20/NY 5 (which soon becomes NY 318). Turn left (west) and drive 2 miles to the intersection with NY 89.

When you reach NY 89, turn right and drive to the Tschache Pool observation tower, just beyond the New York Thruway (I-90) overpass. On your right, you will see the dike road ("M" trail) along the northern edge of May's Point Pool. Start here.

This path is open to the public only from October 1 to March 1, which fortunately allows you to visit during the peak of the fall waterfowl migration. The trail runs just to the tip of the pool, making a relatively short walk of 1½ miles that brings you near the feeding waterfowl. When you arrive at the end, retrace your steps to the parking area to begin your walk on the Tschache Pool

("T") trail, which also starts here.

This second trail, which runs to the northern tip of the pool, is 4¼ miles long. Your walk here is somewhat shorter—only 1¼ miles to the neck of the pool, where the viewing is ideal. On this trail you have an opportunity to get close to the hacking tree.

This pool is a favorite of herons. A common sight throughout the summer and early fall is the great blue heron; you may see as many as half a dozen standing in the water at any one time. June through August is the time for sighting the green heron, which also nests in the refuge. The little blue heron does frequent the area, but it is a rare sight.

After returning to the parking area, drive your vehicle south on NY 89 to Kline Road. Turn right and drive north 1.1 miles to the Esker Brook Trail ("E"); a sign on the right tells you when you have arrived at the parking area and trailhead. Your walk here runs about 2¼ miles, along the top of a glacier-produced esker but mostly through hardwoods. A wooden bench halfway along the trail makes a nice place to stop for a rest. It is also an ideal place to observe birds. Wood thrushes, vireos, veerys, and warblers are especially abundant here in late May and early June.

There are two other hiking trails in the refuge. One is short but attractive, running ½ mile along the southern edge of South Spring Pool. This footpath ("S" trail) is easy to spot from NY 89; a sign points to the entrance.

The Clark Ridge Overlook is the destination of the "C" trail. It is reached by driving north on Kline Road 1.6 miles beyond the Esker Brook Trail parking lot. The less than a mile walk to the overlook is especially pleasant during the summer and fall.

28

Klondike State Forest

Total distance: 5 miles
Hiking time: 2½ hours
Vertical rise: 630 feet
Map: USGS 7½' Panther Lake

Klondike State Forest, although relatively small, is a delight to hike; it provides you with a wooded landscape, varied terrain, an attractive pond, and several easily accessible roads that allow you to walk through the entire forest, as well as to several remote spots in the forest.

Its name makes you think of the cold and forbidding Klondike region in the Yukon district of Northwestern Canada, site of the greatest gold rush the world has ever known. There is little the state forest has in common with its northern namesake, though. It takes its name instead from a low swampy area tagged as "The Klondike" for reasons that are now forgotten. This piece of wetland lies in the northern part of the state land.

The small, 875-acre state forest is located about seven miles north of Oneida Lake between the hamlets of West Amboy in the north and North Constantia in the south. It is situated in what is known as the Oneida Lake Plain, which in turn is in the Ontario Lowland Region.

This low-relief land was once part of an old glacial lake bottom thousands of years ago. The area's low rolling hills consist primarily of ground moraine deposits left behind by the retreating glacier of the Pleistocene period. Because the land is poorly drained, it is dotted with numerous swamps and shallow ponds.

On the southern edge of the state forest are two such ponds—Chase Pond and South Pond, both located on posted private land. To the west, with the state property line passing through its eastern part, is North Pond. Immediately north of the state land is the swampy area known as "The Klondike," whose water drains into North Pond.

The highest spot in the state forest is Chase Hill with an elevation of 673 feet. While the hills are not high, the region has an abundance of rolling terrain that adds variety and attractiveness to your hike.

Access. The state forest lies south of NY 69, which runs east and west between Parish and Camden. NY 69 can be reached easily via I-81, exiting onto NY 69 at Parish (about 22 miles north of Syracuse). Once on NY 69, drive east seven miles to West Amboy. Continue one mile beyond West Amboy to where Tanner Road—a two-lane dirt road—intersects on the right. Turn here, and follow Tanner Road for 1.8 miles to the intersection with Starks Road, a single-lane dirt road. Park here.

Trail. What was once just a walk trail has been widened into a single-lane dirt road

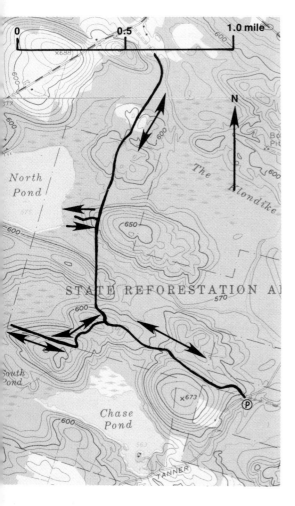

break in the stone fence and up a slight rise. The ascent is a modest one, and after 100 yards the trail levels out as it passes through a stand of pines.

Suddenly the trees give way to a large field on your left. You are now on top of Chase Hill, which gives you an attractive overlook across the field to the southeast. The field pitches gradually downward toward a house at the far end. Hidden from view, but located in the shallow valley to the west, is Chase Pond. Far ahead to the east is tree-covered high ground, with a couple of houses visible in the distance.

Retrace your steps to the road, and continue your hike to the west. In the next ½ mile, the road dips and rises several times; it then turns to the right (north) and heads gradually downhill. At the turn, a jeep trail runs uphill (south). Take the jeep trail for a short excursion to the southwestern corner of the state forest. Once it reaches the top of the hill, it makes a short but sharp descent, only to climb a second hill, at the top of which you meet posted signs indicating you have reached the southern boundary of the state forest.

Intersecting from the right, however, is another jeep trail, parallelling the state boundary line. Turn here, and follow this trail for a little less than ½ mile, until the trail ends as it reaches the state forest's western boundary. The jeep trail is canopied by tall trees to make this a most pleasant hike. When you reach the trail's end, retrace your steps to the main road.

The road is now heading in a northerly direction, dipping into a small depression, rising to the top of a small hill, and then pitching more steeply downward, about 0.2 mile from the jeep trail you hiked earlier. Look along the bank on your left as you head downhill; soon you spot a discernible hiking trail heading uphill and west from the road.

While this is not a heavily used trail, its

as a westward continuation of Starks Road. It is here that you begin your hike. Head westward up a gentle slope. After the first 100 yards, the road levels out. On both sides of the road are stands of hardwood, primarily maple, interspersed with evergreens.

About 0.2 mile down the road, you will see a stone fence paralleling the road on the left, about 20 yards away. As soon as you see another stone fence intersecting at a right angle, turn left off the road, and follow a foot-trail south through a

Quiet fall day on the Klondike Trail

outline is clear enough to allow you to follow it; 0.3 mile brings you to the southern edge of North Pond and a nice overlook of this small but attractive body of water. You are also at the western boundary of the state forest, so reverse direction and return to the main road, where you turn left to continue.

As you reach the bottom of the hill on the main road, you cross a small stream draining water from The Klondike swamp to North Pond. Once across the stream, you ascend a small hill. At the top, the woods have been cut back on the right to permit vehicle parking. Across the road from the parking area is a foot-trail, which you can follow as it leaves the road and heads downhill, taking you a short distance to the eastern edge of North Pond.

Back on the main road again, continue northward for almost ½ mile; here the state forest ends and private property be-

gins, although the line of transition is not discernible because all is heavily forested. You can continue following the road to the end of the woods, about 0.6 mile from the state forest boundary.

Here the forest gives way to a field, on the far side of which are several houses at the south edge of a paved road, County Route 26, just short of a mile south of West Amboy. From here you can retrace your steps through the state forest along the main road to your parked vehicle.

Klondike State Forest also is a good spot for such wintertime activities as snowshoeing and Nordic skiing. Snowshoeing allows you to explore several of the jeep trails, as well as several abandoned logging roads radiating off the main road. The rolling terrain is ideal for ski touring, including a number of sporty downhill runs.

Selkirk Shores State Park

Total distance: 3.5 miles
Hiking time: 2 hours
Vertical rise: 120 feet
Maps: USGS 7½′ Pulaski; Park Map

Selkirk Shores State Park is 1,000 acres of forested land fronting Lake Ontario on the west, bounded on the north by the Salmon River and on the south by Grindstone Creek. The state park has many natural assets that make it an attractive setting for hiking.

You can do a lot of other things here as well—swimming, sailing, canoeing, picnicking, camping, and fishing, more than can be crammed into one day. It is best to plan a weekend outing, or even a longer one.

Like all state parks, Selkirk charges an entrance fee, and if you plan to camp there is a daily camping fee. But you get a lot for your money. Both Grindstone Creek and Salmon River are popular fishing streams. Trout running up to 20 pounds can be found here, including brown trout and Coho and Chinook salmon. More recently the state has begun stocking lake trout and Atlantic salmon in the lake.

The lower reaches of both streams also can be canoed, and of course Lake Ontario is ideal for sailing. The parking area that adjoins Grindstone Creek serves as a boat launching access.

The entire park is woodland right to the water's edge, and most of it is evergreens, with rows of Scotch pines, large stands of tall hemlocks, and a number of spruce and pine plantations that keep the park green the year 'round.

In winter, the park is a popular spot for cross-country skiing. Park personnel maintain groomed and marked ski trails that serve well during the summer as hiking trails. If you combine the ski trails with the park's regular hiking trails and road systems, you have over 15 miles of hiking trails.

The park's other asset is its abundance of wildlife. Hunting and trapping are not permitted here, so the park acts as a game refuge sheltering a surprisingly large number of ruffed grouse, varying hare, red and gray fox, and white-tailed deer. If you are on the trail early in the morning, be prepared to meet some of these local inhabitants.

The park has two entrances. The north entrance leads to an area called Pine Grove, next to the Salmon River, where there are a number of three- and four-room cottages rented to the public by the state. Rental applications are taken in January, and cottages are assigned by lottery. Here, too, you find a boat launching site. There is no entrance fee to this section of the park. The south entrance brings you to the areas where you can swim, picnic, and camp, and here a fee is charged.

Access. The state park is on the east short of Lake Ontario, four miles due west of Pulaski. Entrances are on NY 3, which parallels the shore line and runs from Fulton to Watertown. The park can also be reached via I-81; exit at Pulaski, and follow NY 13 westward past the southern part of the town to Port Ontario, where it intersects with NY 3. Turn south on NY 3, and drive 1.6 miles to the park's southern (main) entrance. A mile west on this access road brings you to the ticket booth.

From the ticket booth, bear to your right. This road takes you in less than ¼ mile to a parking area on your right. Park here.

Trail. Your hiking will be primarily on cross-country ski trails that are marked as such. You will see these markers near the northeast corner of the parking area, where you follow a trail east; it parallels the entrance road you used to reach the parking area. This is the Red Trail, the longest of the two loop trails, which run through the central and northern portion of the park. The short loop, the Green Trail, is in the southern part.

In less than ¼ mile, the trail crosses a

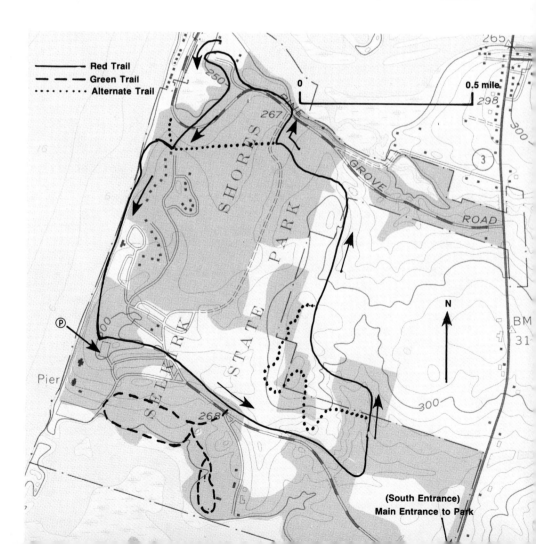

Looking over Salmon River on north side of Selkirk Shores State Park

park road, and then for the next ¾ mile it runs through a wide cut in a stand of Scotch pines, paralleling but well away from the park's entrance road. Soon the Scotch pines give way to a large and impressive stand of red pine. The trail now turns to the left and enters a more open area. To the right are hardwoods and to the left are pines; ahead the field is dotted with small Scotch pines.

A short distance downtrail, you see a marker pointing to a trail intersecting on your left. This is part of the Red Trail's inner loop, which runs about a mile before rejoining the main trail. The main trail soon also turns to the left, heading west for ¼ mile, where it then turns right and runs north; ¼ mile more, and you encounter the second intersection with the inner loop.

In another ¼ mile, the trail turns to the left and heads west. A short distance ahead, you enter an attractive open area and then a stand of tall hemlocks, where you encounter an intersection with a north-south trail. Turn right onto this new trail, and follow it north for ⅛ mile, where it intersects a blacktop road of the park's northern entrance route. Turn left onto the blacktop entrance road, and walk

west ⅛ mile, where a dirt road intersects on the right; en route you see several parking spots among the trees on the Salmon River side of the road, providing some nice views.

Turn right onto the dirt road, and a short distance brings you to Pine Grove with its summer cottages and boat launching site. Retrace your steps to the north entrance road, and continue walking west as the road swings to the left and then to the right; at this spot you should see a hiking trail on your left. You can take this trail or the one further down the road at a spot where the road turns more sharply to the right.

Either of these two trails runs to the south and quickly brings you first to the park's cabin colony area and then to the camping area. Continue southward paralleling the beach to the parking area and your vehicle.

If you have time, you may wish to hike the shorter Green Trail. You pick up the trail markers on the south side of the entrance road about ⅛ mile east of the Park Office, where a service road intersects the entrance road on the right. This trail consists of a western loop and a short eastern loop.

30

Lakeview Wildlife Management Area/ Southwick Beach State Park

Total distance: 9.2 miles (two days)
Hiking time: 5 hours
Vertical rise: Minimal
Maps: USGS 7½' Henderson; USGS 7½' Ellisburg

At first sight of Lakeview Wildlife Management area from NY 3, you see what looks like any other wetland—a large marsh and acres of cattails. There's more here, though, than first meets the eye. While it is true that about 90 per cent of the wildlife area is marsh, the total variety of terrain and vegetation will surprise you. You will encounter a natural barrier beach, high sand dunes covered on the back side with dune vegetation, upland woods, juniper fields, meadowlands, abandoned fields, cultivated fields, conifer forest, and hardwood forest.

The wetland area, 5 miles long and just over 1½ wide, lies between Lake Ontario on the west and the upland (made up of woods and fields) on the east. In the middle is a marsh with a variety of different-sized ponds—Lakeview, Floodwood, Goose, and North and South Colwell Ponds. Here exists a freshwater ecosystem protected from the erosive effects of lake storms by a natural barrier beach with impressively high sand dunes. Feeding this system are several streams—Filmore Brook and Sandy Creek in the north, Mud Brook in the central sector, and South Sandy Creek in the south. All finally empty into Floodwood Pond and thence into Lake Ontario.

This area, then, with its waterways, wetlands, and upland woods, provides shelter for such animals as raccoon, opossum, fox, groundhog, and white-tailed deer; spawning habitat for a variety of fish; and, above all, a breeding, resting, and feeding area for migratory waterfowl, including ducks of more than a dozen species.

Another factor that makes this area especially attractive to the hiker is that Lakeview abuts Southwick Beach State Park in the north. While relatively small compared to Lakeview, Southwick has a large picnic area, an attractive sandy beach, and a dozen camping sites where you can pitch a tent for a weekend stay. The park charges an entrance fee.

As the Lakeview area is an excellent place for long or short day hikes, plan to spend several days camping at Southwick. Together, the two areas provide you with much to see whether you are hiker, naturalist, birdwatcher, or fisherman.

Access. The wildlife area and park are in the southwest corner of Jefferson County, about 10 miles north of Pulaski and 20 miles southwest of Watertown off NY 3. NY 3 can be reached from I-81 at the Pulaski exit, where you drive west on

NY 13 to NY 3 at Port Ontario. From Port Ontario, drive north on NY 3 for 10.2 miles, where Pierrepont Road intersects on the left; this road takes you to Lakeview Pond, a half mile west of NY 3, and to the southern trailhead of the groomed trail system. Continue north on NY 3 for another mile to the intersection with Southwick Road. Turn left onto Southwick Road; 0.8 mile brings you to the entrance of Southwick Beach State Park. If you are planning a weekend outing, make arrangements at the entrance booth for a camping site.

Trail. The northern part of Lakeview Wildlife Management Area that adjoins Southwick offers three miles of marked and groomed trails. You can walk from the state park to the wildlife area or vice versa on trails marked by small white squares with a silhouette of a hiker.

The trailhead to the Filmore Brook Trail is located near the state park's entrance booth, allowing you to enter the wildlife area from the north. The trailhead to the Lake-Meadow Trail is found near the boat launching site at Lakeview Pond in the south. Here you find a small frame building with a sign reading "Lake Meadow Trail" on the east side of the building.

The Beach-Dune Trail starts at the park's western campsite and runs south. It takes you to the wildlife area's 3.8-mile long natural beach, a broad, sandy beach that is restricted to walking to preserve its attractiveness. Many activities are prohibited on this natural beach, including camping, swimming, driving motorized vehicles, picnicking, playing radios or other recording devices, and making fires. If you wish to engage in these activities you can do so in Southwick Beach State Park.

Entering the "natural beach" area

The first day's hiking is on the trail system and natural beach in the northern part of the Lakeview Wildlife Management Area. The second day's walking in the southern half is on a series of unconnected short trails, whose starting points must be reached by vehicle. In three short expeditions, you will be able to inspect the wildlife area from several different vantage points, and in one instance to penetrate into the middle of the marsh area on a trail running on high ground.

First Day.

Southwick Beach State Park to Lakeview Pond and back via the natural beach
Distance: 5.6 miles
Hiking time: 3 hours

From your camping site, follow the blacktop road to the state park's entrance gate, where the Filmore Brook Trail enters the woods on the south side of the road. As you turn onto the trail, you see immediately on your left an abandoned orchard, which quickly gives way to a large hardwood forest. The trail runs south for a short distance, then swings southeast, eventually crossing Filmore Brook at a small waterfall.

The trail now turns sharply to the right, leaves the woods, crosses the southern edge of a cultivated field, runs through a conifer forest, and then enters a hardwood forest to become the Marsh Trail.

In little less than ½ mile, you reach the intersection with the Lake-Meadow Trail, which cuts back sharply to your left. The trail running to the right takes you to the Beach-Dune Trail, which you'll walk later. Turn onto the Lake-Meadow Trail and head northeast.

The next ¼ mile is a trek through a thick stand of hardwood, suddenly giving way to an attractive ¼-mile long meadow and juniper field. The trail, once across this open area, passes through a stand of hardwood, crosses an open area with

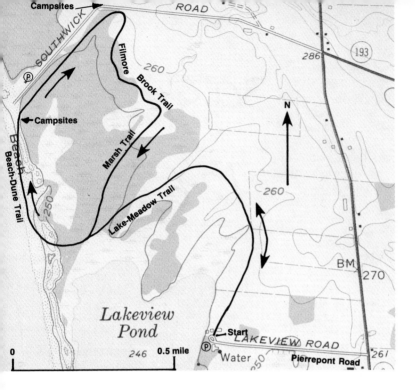

cultivated fields on the left, and then re-enters another wooded area on an abandoned wagon trail.

In ½ mile further, you come to an open area. Ahead you can see a small frame building. As you reach the building you see the boat launching site on the south side and Lakeview Pond on the east. Here, too, you find a large parking area graced by tall trees to provide cool shade as you take a rest break to enjoy the scenery surrounding the pond.

When you are ready, retrace your steps on the Lake-Meadow Trail for a mile to the intersection with the Marsh Trail. On your left is a sign indicating that the trail you are walking will take you to the sand dunes and beach a short distance ahead where the Beach-Dune Trail begins. Continue past the Marsh Trail. Ahead you see the backside of the sand dunes of the barrier beach, as you cross a small brook that at this point is a combination of water from Filmore Brook and

the outlet stream of an unnamed pond into which drain the waters of Southwick Marsh.

As you cross the brook, the hardwoods quickly give way to dune vegetation growing on the east side of what is called the "back dune." A dune area usually is made up of two high spots—the fore dune and a higher back dune with a depression called a panne in between. The dune vegetation stabilizes the dune, preventing the sand from shifting and drifting. Such a stabilized dune area is called a barrier dune, for it acts as a barrier against the wind and storms coming off a large expanse of water, in this case Lake Ontario.

Follow the path over the back and fore dune to the beach. In your walk so far you have come through seven different ecological areas—uncultivated fields, cultivated fields, woods, meadowland, juniper field, dunes, and a natural beach.

This natural beach is quite scenic.

From the water's edge inland, the beach is wide and flat with the sand well packed. The flatness gives way as the dune area is reached; the amount of sand that is piled to form the dunes is impressive, with a fore dune about a story high and a back dune about two stories high. The top of the back dune is covered with trees, predominantly aspen as well as some impressive white pines standing like sentinels guarding the marshlands behind the dunes.

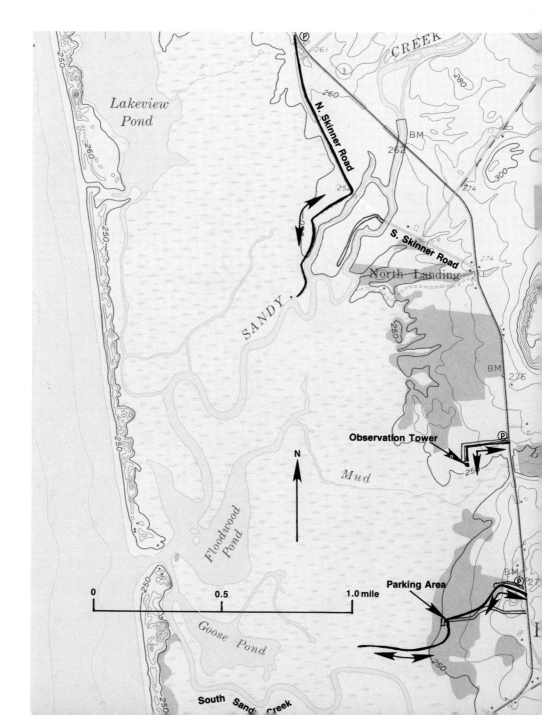

A mile walk south on the natural beach will allow you to better appreciate this unique area. From time to time climb to the top of the barrier dune for scenic views of Lakeview Pond and the marshland to the south.

After your mile walk, retrace your steps north along the beach. Pick up the Beach-Dune trail, and continue north on the beach. In little less than ½ mile, you pass a sign marking the boundary between the wildlife area and the state park. A little further ahead are the beachfront campsites, concession building, and picnic area of Southwick Beach State Park.

Second Day

Southwick Beach State Park to Sandy Creek and the marshland via NY 3
Distance: 3.6 miles
Hiking time: 2 hours

Leave the state park by vehicle for NY 3, and drive south on NY 3 for a little over a mile past Pierrepont Road to North Skinner Road, a dirt road intersecting on the right. Park here. A mile walk along this dirt road will take you to and then along Sandy Creek, one of two main streams that flow into and through the wildlife area. The other is South Sandy Creek.

As you walk along the road you notice that you are on high ground, in an ecosystem typifying an upland environment. While less than ¼ mile to your right is the marsh with vegetation associated with wetlands. After reaching the end of the road, retrace your steps.

Back in your vehicle, drive south on NY 3 for two miles, where a single-lane dirt road intersects on the right. Park here and start your walk going west on

the road; 0.2 mile brings you to a 90-degree turn to the south. A short distance further is an observation tower. From the top you have a nice view of the marsh and, with any luck, you'll see waterfowl taking off, landing or just flying over the marsh.

Head back to your vehicle, and drive south 0.8 mile on NY 3, where another dirt road intersects on the right. Walk west on this road for 0.2 mile to the end, where you can turn south and walk across the field to another east-west dirt road.

Turn west on this dirt road, and follow it to a parking area. A footpath begins at the south end of the parking area. Follow this into the middle of the marsh itself along high ground that has the appearance of a dike. There is water on both sides of the high ground, and, if your timing is good, you may see a lot of waterfowl in the area. Be sure to bring your binoculars.

The predominant vegetation of the marsh is cattails, but the marsh also contains rice cutgrass (*Leersia oryzoides*), pondweeds, arrowhead (or duck potato), bulrushes, bur reeds, sedges, waterweed, musk grass, and swamp loosestrife. A short distance to the south is South Sandy Creek and just ahead is Goose Pond, but all around you is thick vegetation in which red-winged blackbird and marsh wren as well as ducks find protection and a ideal habitat to rest, feed, and nest.

In little less than ½ mile the path ends; retrace your steps to your vehicle and head back to your campsite. If it is summer and the day hot, you can enjoy a swim and the beach at Southwick Beach State park.

Tug Hill

31

Happy Valley Wildlife Management Area

Total distance: 7½ miles
Hiking time: 4 hours
Vertical rise: 1,220 feet
Maps: USGS 7½' Dugway; USGS 7½' Williamstown

Happy Valley is heavily forested, sprinkled with small and large ponds, and crisscrossed with dirt roads, jeep trails, and abandoned logging roads—an ideal setting for short strolls, long day hikes, and even weekend backpacking. Happy Valley Wildlife Management Area is a multi-use area where the State Department of Environmental Conservation emphasizes maintenance of ideal habitat for game such as white-tailed deer and ruffed grouse. Here also one can fish, hunt, snowmobile, cross-country ski, and snowshoe, as well as do some serious hiking.

The state forest covers 8,624 acres of land in Oswego County six miles northeast of Parish on the southern side of Tug Hill. It is the second largest of the four Tug Hill wildlife management areas.

Geologically, it is located in a landform region called the Ontario lowlands, marked by low ridges and swamplands. The North Branch of the Little Salmon River rises here as a small stream flowing south to eventually empty into Little Salmon River.

The two highest places in the forest

View of Long Pond from trail in Happy Valley Wildlife Management Area

are the mile-long ridge officially called Stone Hill (el. 750 feet) and a more peaked hill unofficially called White Hill (el. 700 feet). The latter has the highest vertical rise, 160 feet—a climb that obviously is not very demanding. There are dozens of small man-made impoundments and several large ponds, including almost mile-long Whitney Pond, mile-long Long Pond, half-mile long Mosher Pond, and the smaller St. Mary's Pond.

Spring and fall are the best times of year to hike Happy Valley. May is an ideal month, when the hundreds of apple trees throughout the region are in full bloom. Or pick a time in October for hiking when the fall foliage is at its peak; the splash of color is worth the trip.

Camping is allowed here, and there are some ideal spots along Whitney and Long Ponds. You must obtain a camping permit from the regional office of the DEC in Cortland (607-753-3095). All the large ponds have a good supply of largemouth bass and pan fish, so bring along your fishing gear.

Access. The trailhead can be reached from I-81. Exit at Parish and take County Route 26 northeast for 0.9 miles where it turns right and east. Continue on the

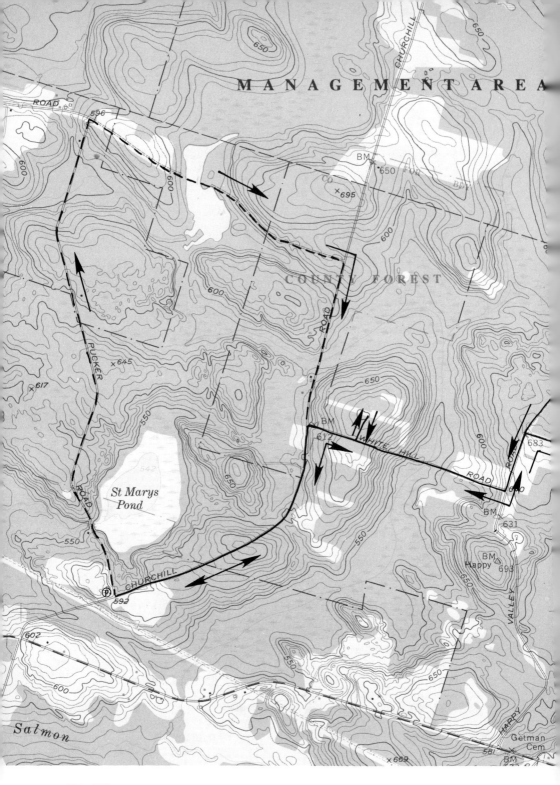

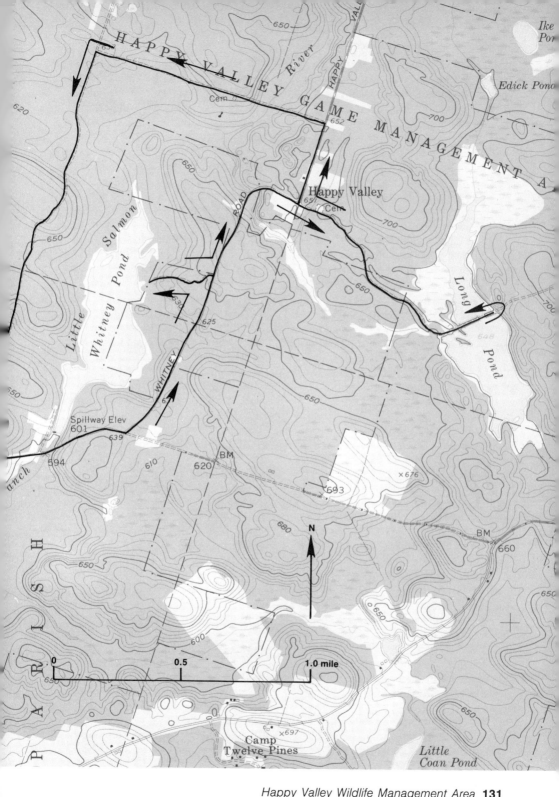

county road for 3.6 miles until it is intersected by Churchill Road, a two-lane dirt road on the left. Drive ½ mile down Churchill Road to its intersection with Pucker Road, and park here.

Trail. There are no marked walking trails on the state land, but you can put together a route combining dirt roads, jeep trails, and fire lanes. Three dirt roads run the full length of Happy Valley from north to south.

At the intersection of Churchill Road and Pucker Road you have two options: the 5-mile Pucker Road-Churchill Road loop, or the 7½-mile Churchill-White Hill-Whitney-Happy Valley Road loop. The latter, while longer, includes the area's two largest and most attractive impoundments, Whitney Pond and Long Pond. Of course, you can shorten this loop by driving to White Hill or Happy Valley Road.

From your parking place, proceed northeast on Churchill Road. The field on your right quickly gives way to woods, and a mile down the road you reach White Hill Road, intersecting on the right. Turn here and head uphill; 0.2 mile and a 70-feet ascent bring you to the top of the hill. The summit of White Hill lies to the left. You can follow the first jeep trail intersecting on the left to the tree-covered top. From the road, however, you have an overlook to the east.

Continue on White Hill Road as it goes downhill and crosses a small brook and then uphill to intersect Happy Valley Road. Turn left (north) here, and follow the road a short distance to a fork, where the main dirt road (now Whitney Road) makes an elbow turn to the right. The left unnamed fork that runs due north probably was once the continuation of Happy Valley Road.

Hike eastward now on Whitney Road for almost ½ mile where you meet another fork. If you turn left, a short distance brings you to the west side of the

Whitney Pond spillway as well as to a fair-sized open area frequently used for camping. At the spillway, you have a nice view north along Whitney Pond. The scenery looks a little like that in the Adirondacks.

Return to Whitney Road, and continue north across the pond's outlet stream (actually the North Branch of Little Salmon River) to a small parking area on the left. From here a path takes you to the east side of the spillway. Back on Whitney Road, a mile walk brings you to a lane intersecting on the left. It leads you in 0.2 mile to the east edge of Whitney Pond, where there's a nice spot to pitch a tent.

Return to Whitney Road again. About ½ mile northward, the road begins to turn to the right (east), and a short distance beyond brings you to a road intersecting on the left (Happy Valley Road). Continue east past the intersection, where you will see a small cemetery with headstones dating back to the 1830s and 1840s, a reminder of the early settlers who transformed forest into farmland. Their community now is completely gone.

Another mile of hiking brings you to a causeway across Long Pond; again the scenery is very Adirondack-like. On the pond's east side, there are good camping spots. You can turn around here and head back to the cemetery.

Just beyond the cemetery, turn right (north) onto Happy Valley Road, and walk for almost ½ mile to where an unnamed dirt road intersects on the left. Turn here and walk west for a mile; en route you will encounter signs indicating state tests on ruffed grouse habitat. At a mile's end, you intersect a single-lane, little-used north-south road. Turn left (south), and in little less than two miles you are back on the main dirt road (the southern end of Happy Valley Road). From here you can retrace your steps two miles to your vehicle.

32

Buck Hill State Forest

Total distance: 11 miles
Hiking time: 4 hours
Vertical rise: 959 feet
Maps: USGS 7½' North Western; USGS 7½' Boonville

Buck Hill State Forest is ideal for a short day hike. To add a few more miles to your trek and to enjoy some additional vistas from this high region, you can include Buck Hill's next-door neighbor, Clark Hill State Forest. And if you're contemplating a weekend camping trip, you might as well include Penn Mountain State Forest, a few miles to the east (see Hike 33).

All three state forests occupy high country making up an escarpment overlooking the Mohawk Valley to the south. Because the land pitches fairly steeply to the south, the high spots provide fine views in virtually all directions of the compass.

Buck Hill is a good example. It is the highest spot in the southern end of the state forest, with an elevation of 1,401 feet. While this height may not seem much compared with some of the other nearby hills, it certainly is enough to give you some fine views to the east and to the north.

Looking northward, you should be able to spot Jackson Hill and, a little to its east, the Boonville gorge, dug out by the large volume of water released by the last continental ice sheet to cover New York as it retreated over 12,000 years

ago. Each of the four glaciers that overran New York contributed to the deepening of the Boonville gorge.

The Pleistocene Ice Age of North American began two million years ago. Four successive glacial advances and retreats were triggered by fluctuations in the climate. As the glaciers advanced, they rounded off hilltops and deepened existing valleys and gorges, and as they melted back they released torrents of water that continued the down-cutting work in such places as the Boonville gorge.

Buck Hill State Forest is relatively small—only 1,494 acres. However, the forest's several truck trails permit you to hike not only to the summit of Buck Hill but also throughout the entire length of the state forest.

Access. Take NY 46 to the village of North Western, which is 12 miles north of Rome and 13 miles south of Boonville. Just ½ mile north of the village is a bridge crossing Stringer Brook; once over the bridge, Buck Hill Road branches east and heads uphill. Follow Buck Hill Road 1.5 miles to the top of the hill where a sign indicates the start of the truck trail. Park here.

Trail. Your hiking here is entirely on truck trails. One such truck road begins on the north side of Buck Hill Road. This dirt road climbs uphill a short distance and then levels out as it loops to the south. The road continues looping until eventually at the ½-mile mark it is heading in a straight northernly direction.

A ½-mile hike brings you to a road intersecting on the right. A short but steep uphill climb takes you to the intersection with another dirt road, running north and south. The land pitches down ahead of you, giving you a fine view to the east as you look over Cyrus Brook and Stringer Brook gorges. A mile to the east you see the forested hilltops of Clark Hill State Forest, specifically Meszler Hill, Maple Mountain, and Oakes Hill.

Turn right here, and follow the road as it takes you south and uphill. In a little less than ½ mile, you reach the summit of Buck Hill. As the road follows the forest edge, the land to the east is open,

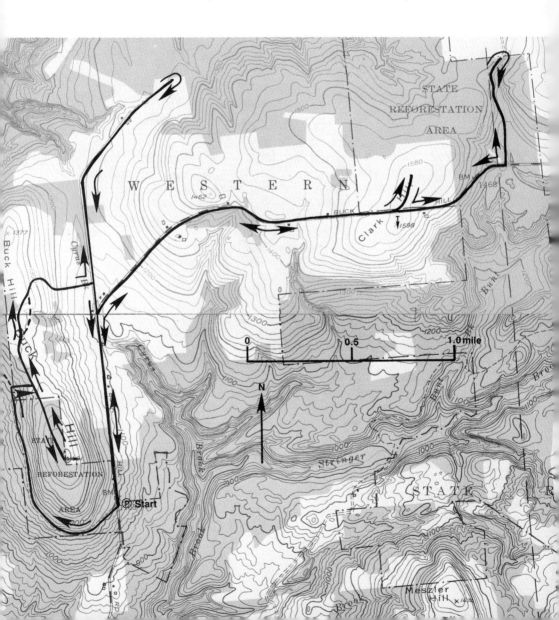

Entering Buck Hill State Forest

giving you some nice vistas. Retrace your steps to the intersection, but continue due north on the road you are hiking.

In ¼ mile you come to a fork. Actually, the road splits here only to come back together again a short distance ahead. This part of the land is level, but soon the road turns right and heads downhill for a little over 1¼ mile to intersect with another north-south dirt road.

Turn left here and follow it northward. This road is relatively level for the first ½ mile; then it turns slightly to the right and begins a gradual descent as it takes you to the boundary of the state land. A little-used lane or jeep trail continues beyond this point on private land. From here you should retrace your steps to your vehicle.

If you would like to add more mileage to your day's outing, you can hike from where you parked your vehicle first north and then east on Buck Hill Road to the summit of Clark Hill, a distance of 2.8 miles.

At the top of Clark Hill, you stand at an elevation of 1,598 feet. The state land is on the north side of the road. On the south side is an open field that allows you an unobstructed view to the south. On a clear day you can see miles from this spot. Here too you find a dirt road leading north into Clark Hill State Forest, but it takes you into the forest only a short distance. If you continue east on Buck Hill Road for another ½ mile, you see a truck trail intersecting from the left. Turn here and walk north; ½ mile brings you to the edge of the state forest and a turn-around area from where you can now retrace your steps to your vehicle.

33

Penn Mountain State Forest

Total distance: 10 miles
Hiking time: 5 hours
Vertical rise: 1,320 feet
Maps: USGS 7½' North Western; USGS 7½' Boonville

If you're looking for a large, peaking mountain similar to those found in the Adirondacks, Penn Mountain won't measure up. Yet compared to the other hills in this region, Penn Mountain is the big fella, with a commanding view of the local countryside.

Penn Mountain is actually a knob on top of the high terrain that makes up the escarpment overlooking the Mohawk Valley, 15 miles to the south. This knob, once the site of a firetower, is 1,813 feet high, a good-sized hill for these parts. It occupies the northern part of the 2,646-acre state forest that is named after it.

The state forest includes several other hilltops—Bowen Hill (el. 1,773 feet), a little over a mile to the southwest of Penn Mountain, and Starr Hill (el. 1,793 feet), at the southern end of the state forest. These last two give you fine overlooks to the west and to the south. Penn Mountain itself is tree-covered, so visibility from there is a bit restricted. However, if you walk a short distance east of the old firetower site on Penn Mountain, the forest ends and you have a view to the east.

Geographically, Penn Mountain State Forest sits between the Tug Hill region in the northwest and the western Adirondack foothills in the northeast and between the Black River Valley in the north

and the Mohawk River Valley in the south.

This land is the source of several streams that feed into the upper reaches of the Mohawk River in the west. It also serves as a watershed, directing the waters of Stringer Brook and Big Brook to the west into the Mohawk and the waters of Cincinnati Creek to the east into West Canada Creek.

Penn Mountain State Forest has several close neighbors that also appeal to hikers—Buck Hill State Forest (see Hike 32) and Clark Hill State Forest, about two miles to the northwest. Just south of Clark Hill State Forest, in the Boonville gorge, is Pixley Falls State Park, a delightful place to picnic and take short hikes.

Access. Penn Mountain State Forest is reached most easily via NY 12/28 for 20 miles to an intersection with a road running west out of the village of Remsen, which is itself a short distance east of NY 12/28.

On the left side of the road you see a sign directing you to Steuben Memorial. Turn left here, and drive west 0.6 mile, where a road intersects on the left. Turn here, and drive south for another 0.6 mile, where a road intersects on the

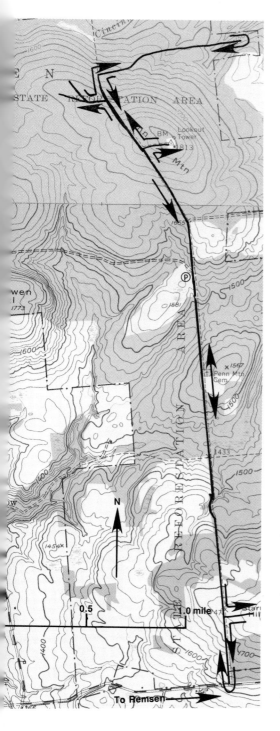

right; take this road, and drive west 3.1 miles, where NY 274 intersects from the south. Continue straight ahead on what has now become NY 274 for a mile, which brings you into the hamlet of Steuben. Turn right here, and drive north four miles to the top of the hill. On your right (east) is a dirt road that takes you into the state forest.

Take this dirt road, and drive east 1.4 miles, where you intersect with another dirt road. Park here.

Trail. The high terrain gives you a number of excellent overlooks beginning at the highway-dirt road intersection. On the way into the state forest, you drive on the northern edge of Bowen Hill, whose crest is about ¼ mile south of the road. A mile to the west is Clark Hill State Forest with its several hills—Oakes Hill, Maple Mountain, and Meszler Hill. As the land descends steeply to the south, you also have a fine view in that direction.

At the spot you parked your vehicle, you find a large open area immediately south of the road. Here too you can enjoy a fine vista to the south. After enjoying the sights, you can begin your hike, which is on dirt roads and truck trails.

At the intersection, turn left on the north-south dirt road, and head north uphill. A little less than ¼ mile brings you to another dirt road intersecting on the right; take this road, and walk east for a little less than ½ mile. This brings you to the edge of the state forest and to open country where you have a good view to the east.

Retrace your steps to the main dirt road, and continue your hike north for ½ mile to where a lane intersects on the right; turn here to go to the site of the old firetower on the crest of Penn Mountain. Back on the main road, continue walking north. The terrain here is level for the next ¼ mile, where you intersect with

*View to southwest from Starr Hill in Penn Mountain State Forest toward
Meszler Hill*

a truck trail on the left. This does not go into the forest very far before it forks, with each leg of the fork running a short distance to a turn-around area.

Returning to the main road, you now start a gradual descent as you continue north for a little less than ¼ mile; here the road turns east. If you proceed straight ahead and down a steep hill, you soon encounter an impoundment — an elongated pond containing the water of Cincinnati Creek, which starts about ½ mile to the west.

Continue on the dirt road toward the east, and a little under a mile further brings you to the road's end. From here you retrace your steps to your parked vehicle to hike the southern portion of the state forest. Stay on the same north-south road. After heading downhill ¼ mile, you start a modest climb for another ¼ mile. When you reach the top, you notice headstones in an open area on your left:

Penn Mountain cemetery, where earlier residents of this land are buried.

The road now begins to slope downward, and in little less than ½ mile you are in a small valley with a lane crossing the road. Continue due south on the main dirt road; soon you cross two spots where, in early spring, you find the headwaters of Big Brook.

The road now runs uphill. It is a steady climb for the next ½ mile for a vertical rise of 214 feet. When you reach the top, you can take the lane on your left to the top of Starr Hill, where you can enjoy a fine vista to the south. If you continue south on the main dirt road for a little over ¼ mile, you will intersect with an east-west highway marking the end of the state forest. The view here to the south is also good. From here you can retrace your steps to your parked vehicle.

34

Mad River State Forest

Total distance: 8.5 miles
Hiking time: 5 hours
Vertical rise: 1,400 feet
Maps: USGS 7½' Florence; USGS 7½' Westdale

In Mad River State Forest you can do some hill climbing. Florence Hill and Wickwire Hill dominate the landscape. You reach the top of Florence Hill (el. 1,074 feet), the highest spot hereabouts, by making an ascent so gradual that you are hardly aware you're doing any climbing at all.

Wickwire Hill is another matter. At 1,060 feet, it is not quite as high as Florence Hill, but it is peaked with steep sloping sides that will make you well aware of climbing. The distance from the trailhead at Mad River to the top of Wickwire is a little less than a half mile—far enough to make the climb challenging but not tiring.

The state forest is located on the southern edge of the Tug Hill region on land that rises fairly abruptly from the Oneida Lake plain in the south. Most high places here are merely bumps on the landscape, but Wickwire Hill, which from a distance stands out distinctly, has a personality all its own.

The 2,700-acre state forest, something of a crazy quilt in layout, takes its name from Mad River, which tumbles down from the higher terrain in the north and rushes through the eastern portion of the state forest. Those who named rivers in

this part of New York were either overly fond of the name "Mad River" or confused, for there are two Mad Rivers in the Tug Hill area. One, which has its beginnings in the central region of Tug Hill, flows south for ten miles to empty into the west-flowing Salmon River. Little over a mile south of the Salmon River Reservoir, you find the headwaters of the second Mad River, the one we refer to here. It too flows south beyond the Mad River State Forest to empty into the East Branch of Fish Creek in Camden.

The state forest is about three miles north of Camden and easy to reach from NY 13. Farmland here is confined to space along the main highways in the area surrounding the state forest. Otherwise, about 85 per cent of the land is thickly forested, so the region has more of a wilderness feel than a cultivated appearance.

There are no designated hiking trails in the state forest, but instead a single-lane truck trail that runs through the central section, with several roads radiating off it. All are wellshaded during the summer to make walking a pleasure. The Erie Bridge Ski Center at the western edge of the state forest provides year-round lodging, and those who stay here during the summer months can hike the network of ski trails that ties into the state forest road system.

Access. Either NY 13 or NY 69 brings you into Camden. At the traffic light in the center of Camden, drive north on NY 13 four blocks to where the road forks. NY 13 bears to the left. Take the right leg, which is Empey Avenue, where you will see a sign to the village of Florence. Follow Empey Avenue north out of Camden; as soon as the road crosses Mad River on the edge of town, its name changes to River Road.

Drive north on River Road for 3.6 miles, where the road crosses Mad River for the third time since leaving Camden. From the bridge continue north for 0.3 mile, where a single-lane dirt road intersects on the left (on the corner is a house). Pull off River Road and park.

Trail. You begin your hike by turning onto the dirt road. A couple hundred feet brings you to a bridge crossing Mad River. Once across the bridge, you enter the forest. Immediately on your right is a small house, the last one you'll see before the state forest, which starts a short distance uphill.

As the road passes the house, it

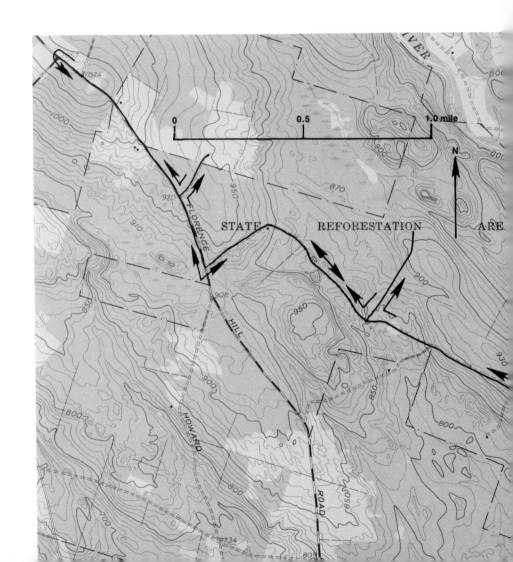

swings a little to the right and heads up-hill. Looming high on your left is Wick-wire Hill. About 0.2 mile uphill, you see a broad, well-used trail intersecting on your left, which has been made by users of all-terrain vehicles (ATVs). On weekends you may see ATVs on this trail, but dur-ing the week usually you can have it to yourself.

The climb to the top of Wickwire Hill is relatively short—only 0.3 mile from the truck trail—but it is fairly steep, especially as you approach the top, with a vertical rise from the trail to the summit of 260 feet. Near the top, the trail forks. Bear to your left, and follow this trail to the hill's

top. The trail turns right, runs a short dis-tance along the narrow ridge, and then loops right and heads downhill to inter-sect the second trail coming uphill. Turn left onto this trail and follow it to the top, where the trail makes a tight loop.

The top of Wickwire Hill is completely forested. During the summer, you don't have much of a view, but in early spring or late fall you'll be able to see to the west.

Retrace your steps downhill to the truck trail, and turn left. Continue your uphill hiking for a little over ¼ mile, at which point the road flattens out, making walking easy for the next ½ mile. At the 1.6-mile mark, a small open area ap-pears on your left. In summer, the area is grassed in, but you might discern the outline of a trail that would take you back into the forest and onto the private land of the Erie Bridge Ski Center. This is the trail that connects the state forest with the Center's cross-country ski trails.

For now, continue on the truck trail in a northwesterly direction. The terrain now becomes more uneven, with the road dipping down for a short distance and then rising to climb the next ridge; ¼ mile more brings you to an intersection with another single-lane dirt road coming in from the right.

If you wish to add a little more distance to your hike, follow this road as it runs al-most due north. It forks in ½ mile, and you can stop and reverse direction. Once back on the main truck trail, turn right and continue on your northwesterly route.

At the intersection, the road dips once again, and a short distance beyond it crosses a wooden bridge over a small brook. At ½ mile from the bridge, the road makes a sharp turn to the left to head southwest. In 0.3 mile, you emerge onto a blacktop highway, Florence Hill Road.

To reach the top of Florence Hill, turn right and head uphill; 0.3 mile brings you

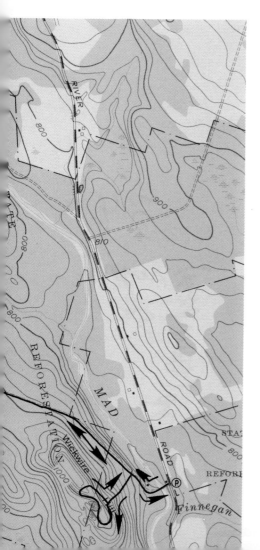

Old stone fence paralleling trail in Mad River State Forest

to a dirt road intersecting on the right. Turn down this road, which ends at 0.2 mile where two gates indicate that the state land has ended. This is a nice spot to take your lunch break.

Back on the blacktop highway, continue north for another ½ mile. You are now on top of Florence Hill. There is a house on your left; between it and the trees lining the road there is an open spot, giving you a fine longdistance view to the south and west.

Continue on the highway for another 0.2 mile, where another blacktop road intersects on the left. At this intersection with Westdale Road, you have a nice overlook to the west before you retrace your steps to your parked vehicle.

35

Chateaugay State Forest

Total distance: 5 miles
Hiking time: 2½ hours
Vertical rise: 240 feet
Map: USGS 7½' Orwell

Chateaugay is a land of tall pines, white-tailed deer, rocky soil, and stone fences. In summer it is full of ferns, acres and acres and all kinds of them—wood ferns, bracken ferns, sensitive ferns, ostrich ferns—soft green in the sunlight that slants through the forest canopy.

It is the stone fences that give Chateaugay its special character; they are a reminder that what is today a dense forest was once farmland. It was hard farming, however, in what is still rocky soil. Some of the rocks are rounded and polished, shaped long ago by glaciers; others are flat and angular, unearthed by the plow only a half century ago.

Whoever built the stone fences did so with care and patience, piling and fitting each stone snugly to make the fences almost a work of art. These fences were the boundaries of small square fields. Given the stony land, you can't help apreciating how much toil and sweat went into keeping these fields cultivated.

That's all past now. Hardwoods and tall conifers have replaced the grain fields and hayfields, and the stone fences now have only trees for neighbors. In this wild forest, the stone fence seems to exert a taming effect on the environment. The

swales of ferns, which cover the ground everywhere, give the forest an even more groomed appearance.

Chateaugay has two more attractions for the hiker—water and a walking trail. Two small but attractive streams, Pekin Brook and Orwell Brook, give the woods the soft sounds of water splashing over rocky ledges and into quiet pools. You can savor all this when you walk the several loops that make up Chateaugay's trail system.

The trail system, built in 1978-79 under the sponsorship of the Oswego County Cooperative Extension Service, was constructed for cross-country skiing. In winter, when the snow lies deep in the state forest, this becomes a skier's mecca. In the off-seasons of spring, summer, and autumn, the trails are ideal for hiking. They can be used either for a day's trek or for an overnight backpacking outing. In the northern part of the state forest about two miles from the trailhead you'll find an Adirondack-style lean-to, should you come to Chateaugay for a weekend.

Access. Chateaugay State Forest can be reached via I-81 by exiting at Pulaski or from US 11, which runs through Pulaski village. Find County Route 2 on the east

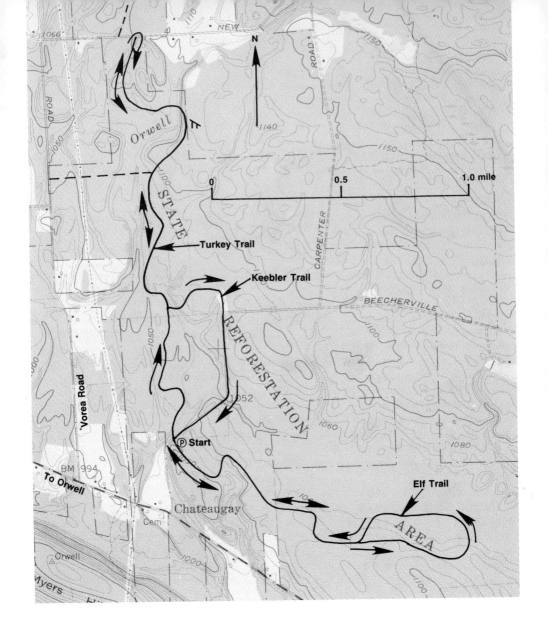

side of the village, and drive east 5.7 miles past Richland to the hamlet of Orwell. From Orwell, continue east for 1.8 miles where Beecherville Road intersects from the left, across from a small cemetery. Drive north on Beecherville Road (a dirt road) for 0.2 mile to a small parking area on the right. Park here.

Trail. Two trails, one running north, the other east, start at the spot where you park. The Chateaugay ski trail system is groomed and marked by yellow discs with a silhouette of a skier. Also, red, yellow, and blue plastic strips are tied around trees to help the skier (or hiker) follow the various trails.

Cross the road and enter the path on the west side of the road, where you will see a signboard with a map of the trail system. The trail on which you are hiking now runs due north two miles; it is designated "B" and called the Turkey Trail. Off this trail loops the mile-long "C" or Keebler Trail. On the east side of Chateaugay (where your car is parked) is a trail designated as "A," the Elf Trail, a little over 1.7 miles long.

Four unmarked trails that radiate off the Turkey Trail can be used for skiing or hiking also. They are not shown on the map here, so if you try them be sure you have map and compass with you. Chateaugay also has several truck trails (Beecherville Road and Carpenter Road) that tie into the ski trails and can be used for hiking. The land is relatively flat with a few small hills that don't rise more than 50 feet.

A short distance downtrail you cross a narrow wooden bridge over Pekin Brook, and in less than 50 yards from the bridge you see your first stone fence on the left. The trail follows along the stone fence for 100 yards, where you turn left and pass through a fence opening. You are now in a stand of pines, and the trail continues north, this time with the stone fence on your right. A short distance ahead, you pass through another opening in the stone fence, and soon thereafter through two more openings, all about the same distance apart.

The trail now intersects the fifth stone fence. Turn left here, keeping the fence on your right and walking through a fern swale. In a short distance, you find an opening in the fence on your right and two signs nailed to a tree on your left.

The sign pointing north indicates the continuation of the Turkey Trail, and the other points to the east at the beginning of the Keebler Trail.

Continue on the Turkey Trail, where just ahead is another wooden footbridge at the foot of a small slope. Soon you pass through another stone fence opening on your right, and in a short distance through the last one. You are now almost a mile uptrail, and the path turns left and then right, bringing you to Orwell Brook.

In spring the brook is full and running swiftly, but by mid-summer the water flow is reduced considerably. Continue along the east side of the brook for ½ mile, and then the trail turns eastward away from the brook. In less than ¼ mile, the path forks. To the right and uphill a short distance, you see the lean-to.

To the left, the trail continues westward over another wooden footbridge into a clearing. Turn to the right here, and follow the markers as the trail swings west again for less than ¼ mile and then heads north; a little over ¼ mile brings you to New Scriba Road, a blacktop highway and the end of the ski trail.

Retrace your steps 1½ miles to the junction with the Keebler Trail. Turn left onto it, and follow the trail east for a little over ¼ mile to where it intersects a dirt road (Beecherville Road). Continue south for just over ½ mile to the trailhead and your parked vehicle.

If you want to do more hiking, try the 1¾-mile-long Elf Trail, which runs from the parking area eastward. It is best to hike the Elf Trail in late spring before summer growth of the ostrich fern and other vegetation fills the trail to make walking somewhat difficult.

Littlejohn Wildlife Management Area

Total distance: 10.4 miles (two days)
Hiking time: 5¾ hours
Vertical rise: 700 feet
Maps: USGS 7½' Boylston; USGS 7½' Worth Center

Save Littlejohn for autumn when the fall foliage is at its peak. With the sun streaming through the treetops, you'll be walking through a cathedral of color, drenched in bright yellows, reds, and browns.

The 8,022-acre Littlejohn Wildlife Management Area is completely forested; so is the land around it, especially to the east and the south where you find an almost trackless wilderness—no communities, no homesteads, not even any roads. It is solid forest.

This is the "Big Woods" or, as it was once called, the "Lesser Wilderness," about 25 miles wide and 30 miles long, making up 750 square miles of dense, wild forest. Only the local population of bobcats calls it home.

The expression "Lesser Wilderness" served to distinguish the Tug Hill forest from what lies east of the Black River Valley, namely, the Adirondack forest, then called the "Greater Wilderness." Actually, there are more foot-trails in the Greater Wilderness area than in the Lesser Wilderness, which should give you some idea of the latter's remoteness and primitiveness.

Littlejohn holds down the western flank of the Tug Hill wilderness area. Although part of the wilderness, it is not all that intimidating and actually appears friendly. Littlejohn's forest is predominantly maple, with well-spaced trees that allow considerable visibility and a feeling of openness. An additional asset is the flatness of the terrain, which makes your hike an easy one. While it will give you a taste of what this wilderness area is like, Littlejohn is easy to reach and to traverse. Roads penetrate from three directions, and a north-south road runs the full length of Littlejohn.

Topographically, the state-owned area is much like the rest of the Tug Hill region; it is high, with an elevation of 1,400 feet, but as flat as a tabletop. It is the latter characteristic that leads some to speak of the Tug Hill plateau. It is in fact a hill, rising from Lake Ontario (el. 260 feet) to over 2,100 feet in the region's eastern edge so gradually that you are unaware of the climb.

Access. Littlejohn Wildlife Management Area can be reached via I-81 and Smartville. Leave I-81 at exit 39, and drive through Sandy Creek and Lacona, picking up Smartville Road (County Route 15) at the eastern end of Lacona. From here, drive 8.1 miles east through the hamlet

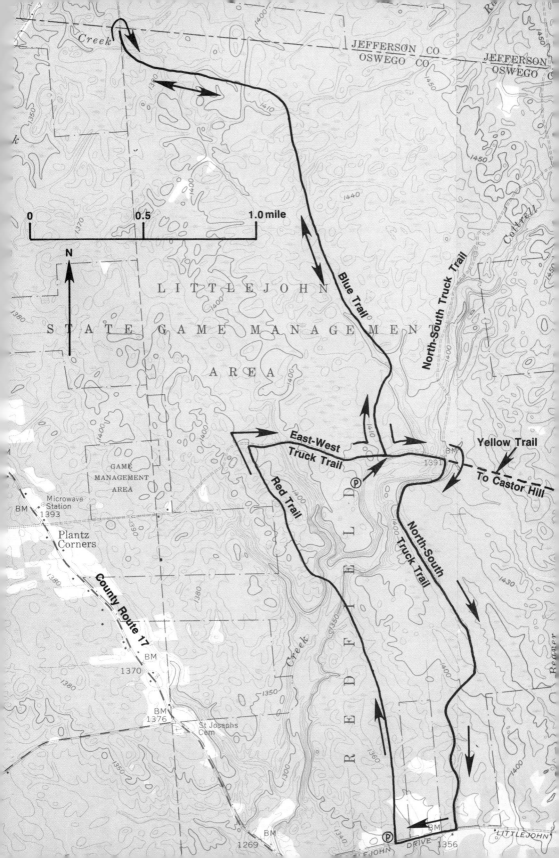

of Smartville to an intersection with the paved Lorraine-Redfield Road (County Route 17). Turn right here, and drive 0.8 mile to where Littlejohn Drive (a dirt road) intersects on the left. Turn and drive 0.6 mile on Littlejohn Drive to a parking area on the left, adjacent to a stand of pines. Park here.

Trail. Littlejohn has several hiking trails and roads that can be combined to make an excellent trail system for the weekend hiker. In the southern part is a two-mile hiking trail marked with red discs. This Red Trail begins where you are parked and runs north to end at what the state foresters call simply the East-West Truck Trail, a one-lane dirt road. The Blue Trail begins ½ mile east on this truck trail. The 2.8 mile-long Blue Trail runs north until it ends at Town Line Road.

Of the two, the Blue Trail is more pleasant to walk in the summer as it is virtually weed-free. The Red Trail, which passes through more open areas and receives more sunlight, soon fills up with weeds as the summer begins. The trail does remain discernible and easy to follow, though.

In the eastern part of Littlejohn is the Yellow Trail. It too starts at Littlejohn Drive on a little rise that, interestingly enough, has a name, Castor Hill (once the site of a firetower). The Yellow Trail ends at the intersection of the East-West and North-South Truck Trails.

To explore several of these trails may require a weekend campout, although any of them will make a good one-day hike.

First Day

Littlejohn Drive to East-West Truck Trail and back
Distance: 4.8 miles
Hiking time: 2½ hours

Begin your hike on the Red Trail. On one of the pine trees at the parking area is a sign reading "Hiking Trail." Enter the pine stand at this point. The trail turns northward and soon crosses a small brook (which usually goes dry in summer), a tributary of Cottrell Creek.

In about 100 yards, the trail leaves the pines and enters an open area that was once a hayfield or pasture and is now slowly reverting to woodland. At the end of ¼ mile, you leave the open area and re-enter the woods. The Red Trail actually follows an abandoned road that may have been either a wagon lane or a logging road.

The terrain is quite flat. If it is midsummer, your travel may be slowed a bit by tall weeds in the lane. You'll encounter some wet spots en route if you are hiking in spring, but by summer most have dried out. At the 1.2-mile mark, you come to a gully where a narrow log footbridge crosses Cottrell Creek. By midsummer the creek is down to a trickle, and you'll have little trouble stepping over what little water remains.

Climb the other side of the gully, and continue on the trail northward as it follows the high ground on the west side of a gully through which flows a tributary of Cottrell Creek. In little over ½ mile, you intersect the East-West Truck Trail. Turn right onto this dirt road and hike east. In ½ mile you come to a sign reading "Hiking Trail" on the north side of the road. This is the beginning of the Blue Trail, which you'll hike later.

For now, continue east on the truck trail, which starts a gradual descent to again cross Cottrell Creek in ¼ mile. Chances are that the water has been dammed by beavers (unless they have been trapped) to create a small pond on both sides of the bridge. On the north side of the bridge about 50 yards away, you will see a huge mound of sawdust, left many years ago by a sawmill that operated around the turn of the century when the area was intensively logged.

A short distance beyond the bridge, you intersect the North-South Truck Trail. Turn right here, and follow the one-lane dirt road southward. The road is well shaded by maple trees on both sides to make this an attractive route to walk. While it makes a number of slow turns, the road is two miles long, the same as the Red Trail. You come out on Littlejohn Drive. Turn right (west), and head back to your starting point ½ mile away.

Second Day

*East-West Truck Trail to Town Line Road
   and back*
Distance: 5.6 miles
Hiking time: 3¼ hours

From the intersection of Littlejohn Drive and County Route 17, drive north two miles to the second intersection. The road on the left is Center Road. The one on the right is the East-West Truck Trail, the main access road to Littlejohn. Drive 1.6 miles east on the East-West Truck Trail to where the Blue Trail begins. There is an area on the right where you can park.

When you enter the woods, you are walking on what looks like a jeep trail, rutted by four-wheel drive vehicles. Don't let this introduction to the Blue Trail disappoint you. A short distance into the woods, the rutted lane gives way to a single path walking trail. It is wide, well-used, easy to follow, and virtually weedless.

In little less than ½ mile, you cross your first stream, a small brook that feeds into Cottrell Creek in the south. A mile of hiking brings you to the second brook, which feeds into Raystone Creek in the north. Your hiking here is on level terrain through a woods of widely-spaced trees, and the trek is a most pleasant one.

In ¼ mile, you come to Raystone Creek itself. In summer, the water is so low that it is easy to cross the creek. The trail now turns gradually to the left and heads in a northwesternly direction. A mile more brings you to the end of the state land and to a turn-around area that marks the southern end of Town Line Road. Retrace your steps on the Blue Trail to the parking area.

37

Tug Hill State Forest

Total distance: 11 miles (two days)
Hiking time: 6 hours
Vertical rise: 220 feet
Map: USGS 7½' Barnes Corners

Tug Hill State Forest is an 11,688-acre tract of state land sprawling in crazy-quilt fashion over the northern slope of Tug Hill and sitting astride the boundary of Jefferson and Lewis Counties. Contiguous to the state forest are 971 acres of Jefferson County Forest. This puts a lot of public land at your disposal and gives you plenty of forested terrain to explore. The big attraction for the hiker is a trail system of loops both in the northern and the southern sections of the state forest.

Actually, the trail system was constructed for cross-country skiers, so you'll find the trail markers to be yellow discs with the silhouette of a skier. These are nailed to trees about eight feet above the ground in anticipation of the winter snows, which in this part of New York come early and in large amounts. Total annual snowfall here averages about 200 inches (over 15 feet), the highest snowfall east of the Rockies.

While the trails are used heavily during the winter by hordes of Nordic skiers, hikers don't use them much during the off-seasons, even though they are excellent for hiking; so you have a lot of trail to follow without someone stepping on your heels. Plan on a weekend trip, covering one section each day. A good time to hike in the area is in late spring or early summer before the weeds grow too high on the ski trails.

The state forest displays many of the features of the Tug Hill region that are something of an anomaly. While it is located literally on top of Tug Hill, the state forest appears to be relatively flat; you'll find no peaked hills or deep valleys here, just a few bumps and depressions. Many of the depressions are soggy, while others are water-filled, producing ponds and wetlands where there ought not to be any. This happens because Tug Hill's sandstone cap is so close to the surface that it prevents water from draining off.

The land may be flat, but there are some surprisingly unexpected gorges that in this region are called gulfs. The gulfs seem to appear out of nowhere, as if some giant had driven a huge axe into arbitrary places throughout the land. The results are deep, straight-walled gorges, some over 200 feet deep.

Inman Gulf, which acts as the northern boundary of Tug Hill State Forest, is a good example. On the southwestern edge of the state forest is Lorraine Gulf, which also will impress you with its depth. When the streams in these gulfs are low in late summer, try walking into one of the gorges as a contrast to walking the flatlands above.

Access. Tug Hill State Forest can be reached from I-81 on the west by exiting at Adams, or from Lowville in the east via NY 177. From Adams, take NY 178 at the south end of the village, and drive east 12 miles to its intersection with NY 177. Turn right onto NY 177, and drive 3/4 mile where you see a large parking area and a small storage shed on the left. Coming from Lowville on NY 177, you will find this area 2.2 miles west of Barnes Corners. Park here.

Trail. Three marked trails begin at the storage shed amid a stand of European larch and red pine. Each ski trail has a name, and some of them are a little unusual. The Home-run Trail follows a truck trail north; the Snowbird Trail runs west; and the Link-up Trail goes south. Two additional loops run off the Home-run Trail: the Whiteway Loop Trail and the Electric Loop Trail. All are well marked with yellow discs, as well as with directional trail name signs and road name signs when a trail crosses a road.

First Day

From Parking Area Loops on Four Trails
  and back
Distance: 5½ miles
Hiking time: 3 hours

At the storage shed, start by taking the Snowbird Trail. Signs for it are found both at the storage shed and on a tree as you enter the trail. A few steps down-trail, you see a sign that this trail was built by the Black River Chapter of the Adirondack Mountain Club.

The Snowbird Trail, which runs for 1.7 miles, parallels NY 177 for ½ mile, taking you through plantations of red pine, white pine, and larch, and then up a small hill. Here the trail turns north, making a gradual descent through evergreens before rising to a knoll of hardwood. It next makes a steep descent

and crosses a footbridge over Fish Creek.

In the next ½ mile, the uphill climb is steady, for a vertical rise of 110 feet. After reaching the top, you then make a short but gentle descent through stands of black cherry, white ash, and beech, until you intersect the Home-run Trail just north of the truck trail.

Turn left and continue north. You go gradually downhill for ¼ mile, cross a tributary of Fish Creek, and pass through a mixed stand of hemlock and hardwood trees. A short distance further brings you to what on the ski trail map is called Times Square, the junction of Electric Loop Trail, Whiteway Loop Trail and Home-run Trail.

Turn left, and follow the Electric Loop Trail, which is 2.2 miles long. It takes you west for almost ¼ mile, where it picks up a Fish Creek tributary. It follows the stream for a while, and at the 0.8-mile mark the trail loops northward, running parallel with the overhead powerline (the Lighthouse Hill Transmission Line) from which the trail takes its name. You follow the powerline for ½ mile, and then swing away from it, heading first northeast and then loops southeast until the trail reaches Times Square.

Here you turn left onto the Whiteway Loop Trail, which covers a distance of 1.8 miles. As the trail leaves Times Square, it passes through a stand of evergreens. At the ¼-mile mark, it turns right to run parallel with the Williams Truck Trail a short distance to the left.

You are now hiking over relatively level terrain. At the mile mark, the trail turns right and goes south for about ¼ mile, then turning right again to run in a southwesterly direction. Soon you climb a small hill, and in about ¼ mile intersect the truck trail that is the Home-run Trail. Turn left here, and head south back to your starting point, which is 700 feet away.

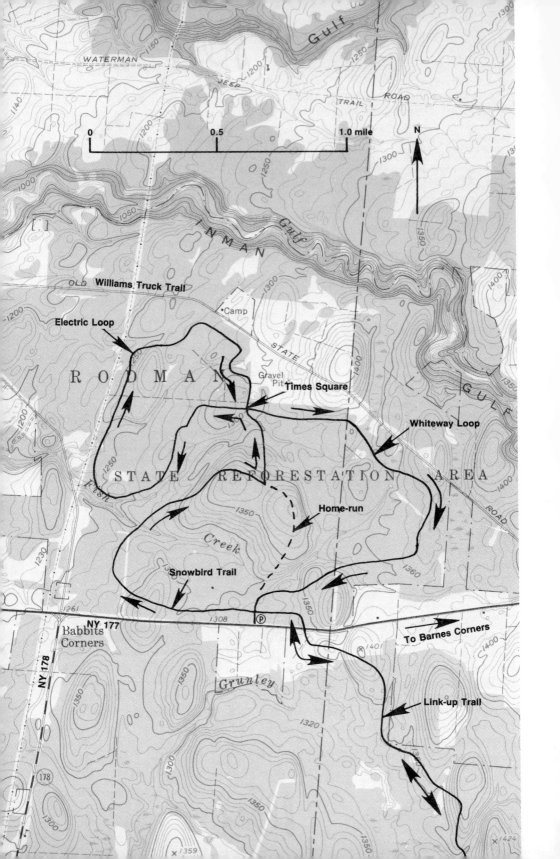

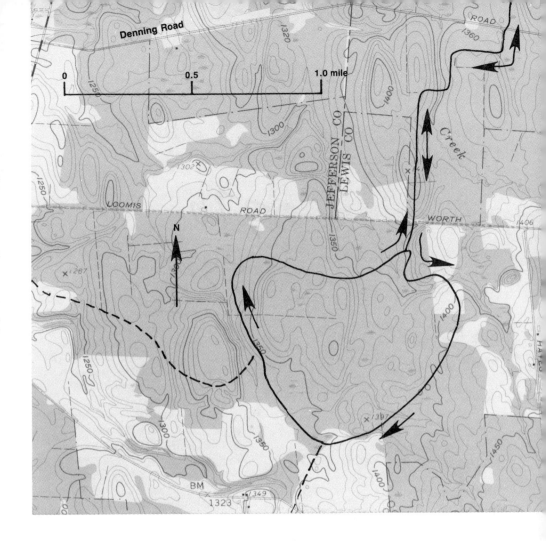

Second Day

*From Parking Area on Link-up Trail and
  back*
Distance: 5½ miles
Hiking time: 3 hours

At the storage shed, a sign directs you to
the Link-up Trail, which runs 2.5 miles to
the south. The trail goes past the storage
shed for a short distance, turns right, and
crosses NY 177. Once across the road,
the trail turns left and heads up a steep
hill for a vertical rise of 100 feet.

At the top, the trail turns slowly to the
right, running over fairly level terrain in a
southernly direction. It passes into an
open area with young white spruce trees,
climbs a small hill, and moves through a
stand of white spruce and white pine.

At the mile mark, you make a fairly
steep descent, cross a tributary of Grunley Creek, and climb a small hill, where
you turn right onto what was once a
wagon road. In a little more than ¼ mile,
you reach a single-lane, east-west truck
trail marked as Denning Road.

Cross this road, and continue on the
trail as it turns right, climbs a hill, and

Entering Tug Hill State Forest

after a couple more turns makes a gradual descent to a bridge over Grunley Creek. A short uphill climb brings you to a ridge that you follow due south for ½ mile to Loomis Road.

This road marks the edge of the state forest; across the road is the Jefferson County Forest, where the trail continues with yellow disc markers. In less than ¼ mile along the trail, you intersect a loop trail built by the Youth Conservation Corps in 1978. Bear to the left, and follow this loop as it heads south to where eventually it is intersected by a trail coming from the south, which in ¼ mile brings you to Waite Road. The main

loop, however, swings in a north-westernly direction, crosses a Grunley Creek tributary, and after ½ mile turns right uphill. It is ¼ mile to the top of this small hill, and ¼ mile more to the lead-in trail that brought you into the loop earlier. Retrace your steps along the Link-up Trail to the storage shed and your parked car.

If you have time and feel a bit adventuresome, try a walk in Inman Gulf. An easy access point is at Barnes Corners 2.2 miles east of the storage shed. From NY 177, turn north on Whitesville Road, and in a short distance you come to a bridge over the Gulf Stream. This is the beginning of Inman Gulf. Enter the gully on the east side of the bridge.

The gully quickly deepens to become a gorge. At the mile mark, the gorge walls run straight up for more than 120 feet. In this short distance, you have witnessed the birth of one of the many gorges that cut deeply into the sides of Tug Hill. Other gorges nearby are Shingle Gulf, a mile north of Inman Gulf, and Bear Gulf, a little further northeast. Through all these gulfs flow streams that eventually feed into Sandy Creek in the western part of Tug Hill.

Still another way to approach Inman Gulf is along the southern rim. Drive west from Barnes Corners on NY 177 for one mile, where Williams Truck Trail intersects on the right. Turn here, and drive 2.2 miles to an open area, where the power-line crosses the road. Walk north on the right-of-way for a little less than ½ mile to the south rim of Inman Gulf. Peek over the rim, and 200 feet straight down you see the stream snaking through the gorge below.

Sears Pond State Forest

Total distance: 16.4 miles (two days)
Hiking time: 8¼ hours
Vertical rise: 920 feet
Maps: USGS 7½' Sears Pond; USGS 7½' New Boston;
USGS 7½' Worth Center; USGS 7½' Barnes Corners

Sears Pond State Forest is an environment in transition: farmland reverting to forestland. Here you are walking through a history of a changing relationship between the land and the people. The state forest also serves as a divide between civilization in the north and east and wilderness in the central and western parts of Tug Hill.

Sears Pond is located in the north central part of the Tug Hill region. This is a region that is surprisingly flat, so flat that you are never aware you are ascending a hill as you drive to the trailhead at the mile-long Sears Pond. Nonetheless, when you drive east from the shores of Lake Ontario to Sears Pond, you go from an elevation of 260 feet to 1,765 feet, for a vertical rise of 1,505 feet.

A little further east of Sears Pond is the Tug Hill escarpment overlooking the Black River Valley; this is the hill's highest point at 2,110 feet, making Tug Hill the highest ground west of the Adirondack Mountain region.

Throughout the 1800s, people pushed up the slopes of Tug Hill in search of more land to farm, cutting back the forest as they went, until finally they reached the top of the hill. Here, however, farming became difficult. The growing season

is short, and the soil is thin and poorly drained—conditions that made farming uneconomical.

In the last 50 years, the farmers have been slowly retreating down the hill and abandoning the farmlands that they had so laboriously attained. The picture of land use today is interesting. On the hill's north slope downhill from NY 177, about 90 per cent of the land is farmed. A few miles south of NY 177 and uphill, only 50 per cent of the land is farmed. In another mile or two, the percentage drops to ten, and as you enter the Sears Pond area less than one per cent is farmed. In this short distance you see an abrupt change in the land's appearance and in the ecological relationships among the land, vegetation, wildlife, and the few human beings who still inhabit the area. The farmers are long gone, and what was once farmland lies fallow, with shrubs and young trees taking over.

To get a good taste of this interesting area, it is best to do it in two bites by hiking two loops. The northwestern loop takes you into wilderness, where all signs of civilization quickly disappear and only a trackless forest remains. The southeastern loop, on the other hand, takes you through the transitional area where peo-

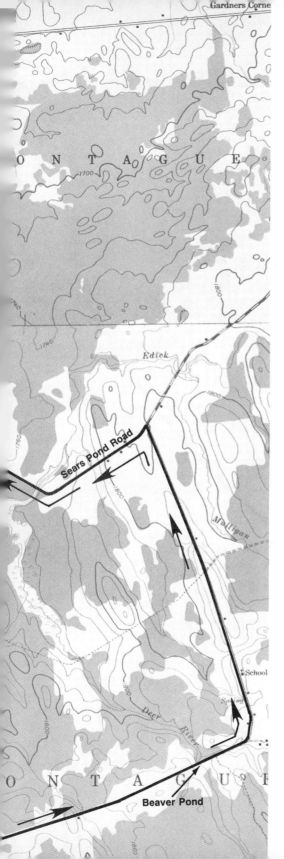

ple still live (many only in summer) and where evidence of past farming can still be seen as the forest slowly creeps back.

Access. The trailhead at Sears Pond lies 6.4 miles south of NY 177. Either from Adams Center in the west or Lowville in the east, take NY 177 to the little hamlet of Bellwood. Turn here onto Sears Pond Road, and drive south until you reach a small parking area near a wooden dam at the north end of Sears Pond. Park here.

Trail. The hiking trails are made up of the several roads and access truck trails that run through the state forest. You can camp in and around the Sears Pond area, with no camping permits required.

First Day

Loop from Liberty Road via Factory Road
Distance: 8.4 miles
Hiking time: 4¼ hours

Begin your hike by walking west from your parked vehicle across the pond's outlet stream to where the one-lane, blacktop Sears Pond Road intersects Liberty Road, another single-lane blacktop road. The outlet stream is really a continuation of the East Branch of the Deer River, which originates several miles south in the Tug Hill Wildlife Management Area (see Hike 39).

Once at the intersection, turn right and head north on Liberty Road for about ¼ mile to where a single-lane dirt road, Worth Road, intersects on the left. Turn onto Worth Road and hike west. You are going through an area that was once farmed, but you will see little evidence of that today, as the forest has replaced the fields. The road parallels the course of the East Branch of Deer River; at the 0.8-mile mark, the road bends a little to the right, and in ½ mile more it turns a little more to the right, coming to the stream's edge.

Sears Pond State Forest **157**

The terrain here is relatively flat, hence the hiking is easy. In slightly under ¼ mile from the stream edge, the road turns sharply to the left taking a due west course. In the next ½ mile, you pass two dirt roads, one intersecting on the left and another on the right, then cross a bridge over the West Branch of Deer River. The second road, Fork Road, is the one you will hike later.

Continue ½ mile east of the West Branch on Worth Road to where another dirt road intersects on the left. Turn here, and follow this road south to an impoundment. You are now on the northern edge of Tug Hill, a wilderness area about 30 miles wide and 20 miles long. Nothing is found here except trees.

Retrace your steps to Fork Road; turn left here and follow it north. At the mile mark, the road crosses the East Branch of Deer Creek, and 0.4 mile more brings you to Factory Road, intersecting on the right. Turn onto Factory Road, and hike east for a mile where you intersect Liberty Road. Turn right, and walk south on this single-lane blacktop road back to Sears Pond and your parked vehicle.

Second Day

Loop from Sears Pond via Pitcher Road
Distance: 8 miles
Hiking time: 4 hours

For the second loop, return to Liberty Road, and follow it south for 2.4 miles. The blacktop road gives way to a two-lane dirt road. En route, you see that the area is quite open, with fields on both sides of the road. You also see more evidence of civilization here, in contrast with the first day; there are quite a few homes along this road.

At the 2.4-mile mark, a single-lane dirt road, Pitcher Road, intersects on the left. Turn here, and hike Pitcher Road eastward. Initially it takes you through a thickly wooded area, but after a mile's walk you leave the state forest and again see abandoned fields on the right. Another ½ mile brings you to a large beaver pond.

The pond extends south from the road for almost ½ mile. The beavers constructed their dam along the edge of the road; it is two feet high, with water spilling over the road. A little over ½ mile down the road, you cross the headwaters of the East Branch of Deer River.

A short distance further, you encounter a cluster of eight houses, most of which appears to be summer cottages. The road bends to the left here and heads north as you re-enter the state forest. Fields on both sides of the road that were once cultivated today lie fallow, waiting for the forest to take over.

From the cluster of houses it is 1.8 miles to the intersection with Sears Pond Road. Turn left here, and follow the single-lane blacktop road as it takes you over Edick Creek, which flows into Sears Pond on your left, then finally to your parked vehicle.

Tug Hill Wildlife Management Area

Total distance: 8½ miles
Hiking time: 4 hours
Vertical rise: 400 feet
Map: USGS 7½′ Sears Pond

Before the farmers and lumbermen came, early in the 1800s, the entire Tug Hill region was heavily forested. It was frequently referred to as the "Lesser Wilderness" to distinguish it from the Adirondack forest region, which was called the "Greater Wilderness."

Today, while the slopes on all sides of Tug Hill are farmed, the region's central portion—600 square miles—is still as it once was, a wilderness. There are no homes, no roads, not even a hiking trail. This is an area of dense woods, virtually impenetrable. No one ventures into the heart of the region, which is more remote and more primitive than any place in the Adirondacks.

Yet you can get a taste of this unusual wilderness by hiking in the Tug Hill Wildlife Management Area (not to be confused with its close kinsman, the Tug Hill State Forest, located about ten miles to the northwest—see Hike 37). The wildlife management area, in turn, is part of the much larger Tug Hill wilderness, which occupies 4,985 acres in the north central part of this wilderness area.

A four-mile long, single-lane dirt road runs through the central part of the wildlife management area, with a foot-trail continuing a mile beyond the road. This allows you to walk from one end to the other of this large parcel of state land.

En route you pass a large, mile-long impoundment and cross two streams that make up the headwaters of the north-flowing Deer River. The land of the game management area is also a drainage area. From the top of Tug Hill at an elevation of 1,900 feet, the land drains water into the Deer River flowing north, Mad River flowing west, and Fish Creek flowing south.

It is the home of the white-tailed deer, red and gray fox, Eastern coyote, fisher, bobcat, and an occasional stray black bear that wanders into the area from the western Adirondack foothills. Here and there on beech trees you can see old claw marks of such a visitor. The deer here are not present in plentiful numbers, and in winter they move southeast to lower elevations to yard in what is called the Highmarket area, where the snow is not so deep.

The predominant trees are beech and red maple. Mixed in with the hardwoods are fairly large stands of conifers, primarily pine, spruce, and hemlock. Also found here is the relatively rare black spruce, variously called "bog spruce" or "swamp spruce." This is the environment for it, with a number of large bog and swamp areas throughout the area.

If you are a bird-watcher as well as a hiker, you will enjoy hiking here, for the

area has received high marks by birders, especially in spring and autumn. Here you see yellow-bellied and least flycatchers, kinglets, cedar waxwings, hermit thrushes, mourning warblers, and white-throated and Lincoln's sparrows, not to mention migrating waterfowl. Goshawks nest here, and so do several different species of owls. Late spring and early summer, when the woods are full of wild flowers, is the time for spotting northward migrating hawks.

Access. The wildlife management area can be reached most easily from NY 177, which runs along the north slope of Tug Hill between Watertown and Lowville. About ten miles west of Lowville is a cluster of several homes that make up the hamlet of Bellwood. Turn south here onto Sears Pond Road; continue on this road for 3.6 miles to Rector, where Sears Pond Road turns right. Straight ahead, however, a dirt road (Parker Road) continues due south. Follow Parker Road for 1.8 miles to its intersection with another dirt road (Flatrock Road). Here you will see a sign that you are entering the Tug Hill Wildlife Management Area. Park here.

Trail. The single-lane main dirt road takes you to the southwestern corner of the management area. Running off this main route are several access roads, each about a mile in length. You can hike in the area for a one-day trek or for a weekend outing. There is a fairly large open area at the end of the main road that can serve as your camping area.

From the parking spot, the road runs straight in a southeasternly direction for 2.2 miles to the impoundment. The trees have been cut back from the road to make the road look wider than it is. Beyond the impoundment, however, the trees grow to the edge of the road, providing cool shade for the hiker on a hot summer day.

After you have hiked ½ mile down the road, you can detect wetlands lying about 200 to 300 feet off the right side of the road; running through the elongated swamp is a small stream, Mulligan Creek. A mile further brings you to the first of a series of access roads running off the main road. This one intersects on the left. Another lane intersects on the left ½ mile further, and in less than ¼ mile you encounter the third, also on the left.

Continue on the main road for little over ¼ mile, where the road turns right and crosses high ground that dams a large impoundment on the south side of the road. Here you can find various species of nesting ducks; during spring and autumn migratory periods, the pond will be filled with geese as well, as they stop to rest and feed.

Along the road on the other side of the impoundment, a lane intersects on the left; it runs about ½ mile south. Continue on the main road, and in a little over ¼ mile you encounter still another access road, this time intersecting on the right; 0.4 mile further brings you to a small stream flowing over the road, and another 0.4 mile leads you to a second and somewhat larger stream that also flows over the road. In summer the water is about four to six inches deep, and you need high waterproof boots to cross.

A mile more brings you to the road's end and a fairly large open spot used as a turn-around area. A mound of dirt across the road forms a barrier against further vehicular travel. Trail bikers, though, have circled around it to continue south on what is an extension of the main road. This gives you a walking path if you would like to continue your hike further. The little-used road ends in a mile at the wildlife management area's western boundary.

You can now retrace your steps, exploring en route all or some of the access roads you passed earlier.

Whetstone Gulf State Park

Total distance: 4.6 miles
Hiking time: 3 hours
Vertical rise: 567 feet
Maps: USGS 7½' Glenfield; USGS 7½' Page

On a scale running from the commonplace to the spectacular, Whetstone Gulf State Park lies at the top. While throughout the Tug Hill region you find gullies and gorges (called gulfs) cut into the slopes of the "Hill," you can see one of the most impressive examples in this state park.

As gulfs go, Whetstone's is relatively short, only two miles long; what it lacks in length it makes up for in depth. The upper (western) end is narrow and breath-takingly deep. The walls of the gorge go straight down, cut by glacial waters just as a hot knife goes through butter. From the rim's edge, you look down 400 feet to the bottom where the waters of Whetstone Creek bounce over rocks and boulders. Anything this deep really qualifies as a canyon.

What surprises you at first is how so deep an incision could have been made in a hillside that otherwise looks so gentle and benign. That is a characteristic typical of Tug Hill—juxtaposition of the unexpected with the expected, the gentle with the rugged, pastoral cultivated fields with thick forests rimming yawning gulfs. What brings the hiker to the Hill is the search for the unexpected, or still another surprise.

When you plan to hike Whetstone

Gulf's rim trails, you might consider a hike into the park's neighbor, the Lesser Wilderness State Forest (see Hike 41), which adjoins Whetstone Gulf State Park. A dirt road, Corrigan Road, on the western edge of the park's gulf, takes you straight into the central part of the Lesser Wilderness State Forest.

Whetstone Gulf has facilities for camping and swimming, so you can make a weekend of your visit to the area. There is a charge for entering the park, but camping reservations are not required.

As you walk the rim trails, you will notice that the layered rock of the canyon is almost entirely black shale with thin interbeds of grayish siltstone and sandstone; fossils are prevalent in the silty beds. It is the softness of this formation that contributed to canyon-cutting.

The eastern entrance to the park marks the contact between the underlying limestone and the overlying Utica shale; resting on top of the Utica shale is the Lorraine rock group and Pulaski rock formation. These formations are well exposed in the upper end of the gorge.

Access. Whetstone Gulf State Park is located 6.3 miles south of Lowville on NY 26. Lowville, in turn, can be reached via NY 12 from Watertown in the north or

Utica in the south, or via NY 26 from Rome. The park's entrance is on NY 26.

Trail. A foot-trail completely encircling the gorge is divided into the South Rim Trail and the North Rim Trail. Once you are inside the park, signs direct you to the trail beginnings. The South Rim Trail begins on the south side of a recreational building adjacent to Whetstone Creek; the North Rim Trail starts on the north side of the creek. It doesn't make any difference which trail you take, for they join one another at the road at the western edge of the gorge, allowing you to loop back to the park entrance. Let's begin with the South Rim Trail.

Once you are on this trail, it is a steady uphill climb through a forest area that provides cool shade during the hot summer months. At about the ½-mile mark, you will have climbed the steepest part,

View of Whetstone Gulf with its almost vertical walls

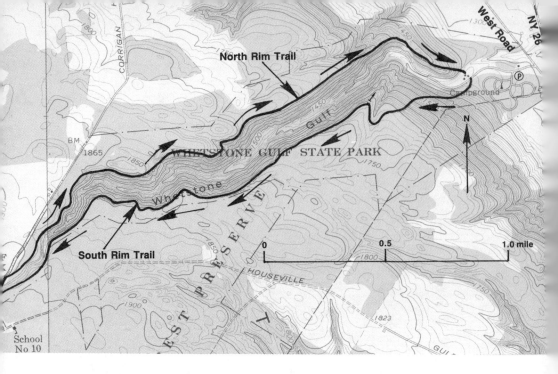

for a vertical rise of 400 feet.

The trail now levels out and then makes a sharp right turn; a short distance brings you to the rim edge, allowing you for the first time to get a good view of this lower end of the gorge. The walls are more slanted here than those you will see at the upper end. A short distance off the trail to your right is a wooden observation platform. From here you have a fine view of the Black River Valley and surrounding countryside to the east.

The trail now follows the gulf's southern rim, letting you look into the gorge as you walk. It continues uphill, with a gradual rise for the next ½ mile, flattening out when you reach the halfway mark. From here on the hike is on level ground.

At about the 1½-mile mark, the gorge begins to narrow and deepen; the walls become perpendicular. You now reach a spot where the trail bends a little to the right, bringing you to a huge boulder left here by the retreating glacier some 12,000 years ago. The boulder sits liter-

ally on the edge of the rim. From this spot you have a fine view of the gorge to the east.

A short distance further brings you to a single-lane dirt road (Corrigan Road). At this point the gorge has been reduced to a gully containing a series of small falls as Whetstone Creek makes its way into the gorge. Turn right onto the road, and cross Whetstone Creek. On the other side the North Rim Trail begins.

The trail on the north is pretty much a repeat of what you saw on the south. The terrain is about the same too; the first mile is relatively flat, and then the trail starts a gradual downhill descent.

At the 1½-mile mark, the downward pitch becomes more pronounced, and the last ½ mile is very steep. Before you start the final descent, the trail turns to the right, or southeasternly. It eventually breaks out of the woods as you reach bottom on the north side of Whetstone Creek. Jumping from stone to stone in the creek brings you to the south side and the parking lot where you left your vehicle.

41

Lesser Wilderness State Forest

Total distance: 9.6 miles
Hiking time: 5 hours
Vertical Rise: 390 feet
Maps: USGS 7½' Glenfield; USGS 7½' Page

The Adirondack Region, which spreads over a vast area east of the Black River Valley, has been called the "Greater Wilderness." To the west of the Black River Valley is a much smaller area on Tug Hill called the "Lesser Wilderness." The state has preserved this old terminology in the name of one of the state forests on the eastern edge of Tug Hill, the highest land west of the Adirondack High Peaks. The Lesser Wilderness State Forest is the largest state holding on Tug Hill — 13,740 acres.

The foot-traveler who calculates distance in what his or her feet can cover in a day will regard this state forest as an impressive amount of territory. Actually it is broken into five pieces with the center-parcel the largest at eight miles wide and six miles long. Connecting roads and jeep trails permit you to hike from one parcel to the next with ease, and, if you have the stamina, from one end to the other — 16 miles one way.

Even though the state forest is located on the highest place on Tug Hill, its topography is relatively flat. It serves as a drainage area for streams flowing to all directions: Roaring Brook, Whetstone Creek, Alder Creek, House Creek, Mill Creek, and the East and North Branches of Fish Creek.

One of the larger parcels of Lesser Wilderness adjoins Whetstone Gulf State Park (see Hike 40). If you are planning a weekend outing, you can combine hikes in the state forest and the state park. The state park includes campsites, so you can make it your base.

The southern half of the Lesser Wilderness State Forest is solid woods. The northern part is a land in transition from farmland to woodland, but the area is still fairly open. In the north, you find Whetstone Creek flowing out of an impoundment that represents one of the largest bodies of water on Tug Hill (at an elevation of 1,902 feet). A couple miles south is Gomer Hill, the highest spot on Tug Hill, with an elevation of 2,110 feet. For a good appreciation of the area's diversified landmarks, plan your hiking route carefully, and try to spend at least a full day.

Access. The state forest entrance on Carpenter Road can be reached via NY 26, which runs from Rome in the south through Turin to Lowville in the north. Carpenter Road is 8.8 miles south of Lowville and 3.4 miles north of Turin. Driving north from Turin, you'll pass the Snow Ridge Ski Center on the left. Where Carpenter Road intersects NY

WHETSTONE GULF
STATE PARK

Graves Corners

McGraw Corners

Creek

School
No 10

STATE FOR

JEEP

TABOLT

BM 1904

Tabolt
Corners

BM
1946

BM
1902

1900

STATE FOR

1909

920

BREN

2000

1950

TURIN

2000

1894

2050

1950

2000

N

0   0.5   1.0 mile

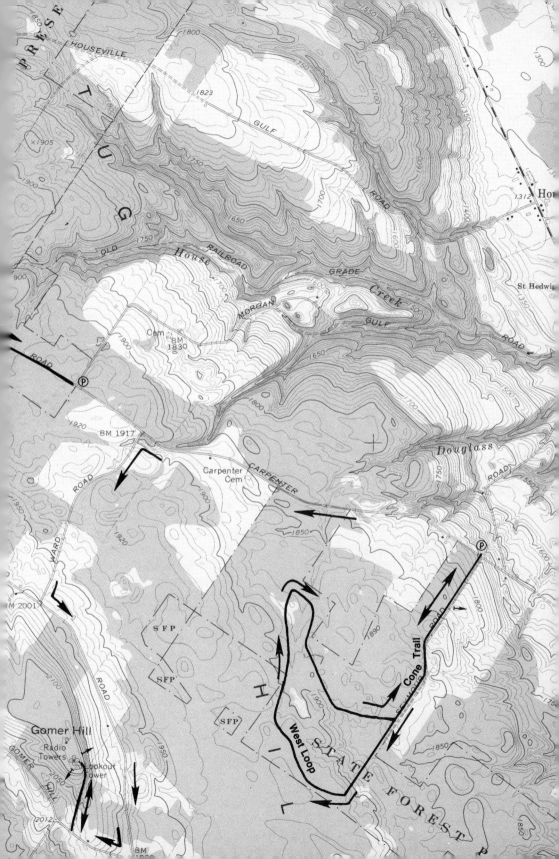

26 on the west, you see a sign to Gomer Hill and to a cross-country ski area. Turn here, and drive uphill on the dirt road for 1.2 miles, where the road makes a sharp turn to the right; 0.1 mile more brings you to a lane intersecting on the left, where there is a sign pointing to the cross-country ski area. Park here.

Trail. Your hiking is broken up into two stages, the first beginning in the parcel with the cross-country ski trails, the other several miles further north. In between you can drive to the firetower on Gomer Hill, where you can climb the tower to enjoy a fine view.

A short distance up the lane from the parking area, you see a booth where in winter Nordic skiers are asked to register. The ski trail parallels the lane on the right. However, weeds grow tall on it, making walking difficult, so stay on the lane (Seymour Road). For a little over ¼ mile it is a gradual uphill climb; another ½ mile brings you to where you can see the ski trail markers on the right; here the West Loop and Cone Trails meet.

For the next ½ mile the terrain is flat; the lane continues straight in a south-westerly direction on the edge of the state forest. Through the trees on the left you can see an open field and beyond it a nice view of the Black River Valley. At 0.6 mile, the ski trail crosses the road, with the West Loop on your right. If the grass in the trail is not too high, try walking this trail. It is two miles long, bringing you back to Seymour Road at the spot you passed earlier. If you decide against the West Loop, you can retrace your steps on Seymour Road to your parked vehicle.

To drive to the manned firetower on Gomer Hill, continue west on Carpenter Road for 1.6 miles, where Ward Road intersects on the left. Turn here, and follow Ward Road south for a mile to its intersection with Brenon Road. Turn left, and follow Brenon Road south for 1.2 miles to the intersection with Gomer Hill Road. Turn right on Gomer Hill Road, and 0.4 mile brings you to a road on the right leading to the firetower.

Another 0.4 mile up this road brings you to the firetower, which is surrounded by five radio towers, part of the Federal Aviation Agency Communication Facility. At the top of the tower, an observer can answer your questions and tell you about the surrounding territory. After you have enjoyed the view, return to your car and drive back to Carpenter Road.

Turn left here onto what is now called Tabolt Road; continue northwest on Tabolt Road 0.4 mile, where another parcel of the Lesser Wilderness begins. Park here.

Begin your second hike by walking west on Tabolt Road, a single-lane dirt road that passes through a heavily-wooded section of the state forest. The trees keep the road shaded and cool in summer. After hiking 0.8 mile, you reach an intersection with two other roads. One, which leads to Whetstone Reservoir, is fenced off; the other forks to the left and runs south. Follow Tabolt Road as it forks to the right; a mile brings you to an intersection with Houseville Gulf Road.

Turn right here, and in a short distance you reach Corrigan Road intersecting on the left. Follow it north for 0.2 mile to where it crosses Whetstone Creek. On the south side of the bridge you find the entrance to the South Rim Trail of Whetstone Gulf State Park. Take this trail to the right, and 0.2 mile brings you to a spot where you can view the narrow, awesomely deep gorge that's called Whetstone Gulf.

Retrace your steps to Corrigan Road and then to Houseville Gulf Road. Turn right and follow Houseville Gulf Road for 0.4 mile, where a lane intersects on the left beyond Whetstone Creek. A short

Field of "erratics" on top of Lesser Wilderness State Forest

walk south on this lane brings you to the impoundment, Whetstone Reservoir, which is almost two miles long.

Retrace your steps to Houseville Gulf Road, and turn left. As you walk, notice that the forest has given way to more open land, which was once farmland. In 0.4 mile, you come to an intersection with an unnamed dirt road (Graves Corners on the topo map).

Turn left, and follow the dirt road west. On the right you have a full view of abandoned farmland that is slowly revert-ing to woodland; at the moment it produces a thick crop of shrubs and small trees. A mile from Graves Corners, you reach another intersection, known in the past as McGraw Corners. The elevation here is 2,000 feet, so you have a fine view to the east and south. In the east the land is fairly open; to the south it is heavily wooded.

Retrace your steps 2.8 miles to your parked vehicle to complete your hike through three portions of the Lesser Wilderness State Forest.

Western Adirondack Hills

Lean-to facing Streeter Lake

Aldrich Pond Wild Forest

Total distance: 17.2 miles (two days)
Hiking time: 8 hours
Vertical rise: 640 feet
Maps: USGS 7½' Oswegatchie; USGS 7½' Oswegatchie SE

At the end of almost a five mile hike into Aldrich Pond Wild Forest are two beautiful lakes—like finding gold at the end of the rainbow. Streeter Lake and Crystal Lake lie a half mile west of Streeter Mountain (el. 1,767 feet), one of the many hills hereabouts that rise above 1,700 feet.

The lakes, a tenth of a mile apart, are quite different. Streeter Lake is five times larger than Crystal Lake. Its water is dark-colored, as is so typical of Adirondack lakes. Crystal Lake, as its name implies, is transparently clear, with a white sandy bottom. The environment in and around the two lakes is also a bit different. Crystal Lake contains no fish; Streeter does. Play the role of naturalist and make a comparative study.

At one time, a large expanse of land surrounding these two lakes was owned by the Shuler family, and it is still frequently referred to as the Shuler Tract. The summer estate consisted of one large main lodge and several guest houses. A large field just north of the buildings was used to raise potatoes for the owner's potato chip business in southern New York.

This field, about ¼ mile square, is certainly an unusual sight in this wilderness region. It is the only open spot for miles around, although it is slowly reverting to forest, as young birch, aspen, and pine trees take root.

And if you don't know its history, the open area comes as even more of a surprise. There is no evidence now that it was once a potato field, much less that it was part of a large estate. All the buildings were razed and/or removed after New York State acquired the land in 1975. All you find here now is a lean-to overlooking Streeter Lake, a short distance from where the main lodge once stood.

When the state took possession of about 4,000 acres of this estate in the St. Lawrence County town of Fine, it closed a gap in the northwest region of the Forest Preserve. The Department of Environmental Conservation has designated the Shuler Tract and surrounding state land as the Aldrich Pond Wild Forest. Adjacent to the area on the east is the Five Ponds Wilderness Area, which surrounds Cranberry Lake.

Topographically, the terrain is rolling, with low hills, exposed outcrops of crystalline rocks, large glacial erratics, bogs and swamps, and a number of streams, including Little River, Tamarack Creek, and the Middle Branch of the Oswegatchie River.

The land now is covered with hardwood second growth that includes sugar maple, black cherry, and beech. In early spring, the forest floor is ablaze with flowers of every variety, making as attractive a scene as can be found anywhere in the Adirondacks.

Because of the low elevation and large number of wetland areas, a sizable deer population exists in the area, so it is a popular place in the fall for hunters, especially those who like to start hunting early in October with bow or muzzle-loader; the rifle season starts later in the month.

In addition to the white-tailed deer, there are black bear, and in recent years moose have been sighted in this general area. A plentiful supply of the large Eastern coyote also is found here. Among the smaller mammals are fisher, beaver, porcupine, raccoon, and varying hare.

Access. The trailhead is found at the southern edge of the village of Star Lake. Star Lake can be reached via NY 3 between Watertown and Tupper Lake. In the center of the village, Griffin Road intersects on the south. Turn here, and drive south on Griffin Road for 0.8 mile, where Lake Road intersects on the right. Turn onto Lake Road, and drive west 0.2 mile to the intersection with Amos Road. Turn left onto Amos Road, and drive 0.6 mile to the trailhead, which is on the left side of the road. Park here.

Trail. A sign at the trailhead indicates that the trail to Streeter Lake was built by the Youth Conservation Corps. It is groomed and marked with yellow discs. Once at Streeter Lake, you will continue hiking on abandoned roads that run south from the lake.

The first leg of your hike from the trailhead to Streeter Lake is 4.8 miles. The second from Streeter Lake to the other side of Bassetts Creek is 3.8 miles. To do both requires a weekend, so you should plan to backpack to Streeter Lake and stay overnight at the lean-to. On the other hand, the route to Streeter Lake and back makes a good day trek.

First Day

From Amos Road to Streeter Lake
  Lean-to
Distance: 4.8 miles
Hiking time: 3 hours

Your hike starts with a short downhill descent. Thereafter the terrain stays fairly level for the next 0.8 mile, where you cross a wooden footbridge over the slow-moving Little River. Once over the bridge, you intersect another trail running east and west. Turn to your left on what is actually a snowmobile trail, and count off 35 steps. On your right, the Streeter Lake trail continues uphill.

For the next 0.8 mile you have a gradual uphill climb; the vertical rise in this stretch is 200 feet. In the next ¼ mile, you make a gradual descent to a low area and then start a relatively short and gradual uphill climb. The trail slopes downward again, and in less than ½ mile you enter a gully-like area, cross two log footbridges, and pass by several large impressive outcrops.

The first one may remind you of a fortress guarding a valley, the second more of pillboxes guarding the lowlands on your left. A short distance further, you cross another footbridge. The trail now rises, swings to the left, and climbs a small hill, only to turn sharply to the right to make a descent to the north side of Streeter Lake Outlet.

At Streeter Lake is an abandoned single-lane dirt road from the hamlet of Aldrich several miles to the north. Where it crosses Streeter Lake Outlet, a gate now prevents access to the area by vehicle. Although it is no longer open to vehi-

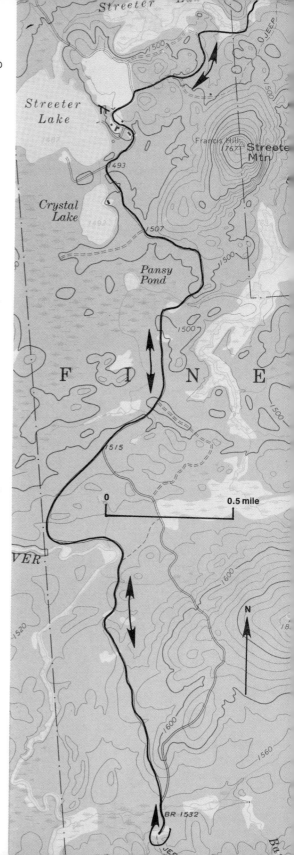

cles, the road still runs past Streeter and Crystal Lakes to end several miles to the south.

The trail runs along the edge of the outlet for a short distance and then crosses it on a wooden footbridge. Once across, the trail turns to the right, heading gradually uphill. In less than 0.2 mile, it intersects an abandoned, weed-filled single-lane road, which is actually a loop that in either direction brings you to Streeter Lake.

For the shorter distance, turn to your left, and follow the road southward. In a little over 0.2 mile, the road, after looping to the east, intersects another abandoned, single-lane road, which in winter is a popular route for cross-country skiers. Another 0.2 mile west on this road brings you to the edge of the forest and the start of the abandoned potato field; the road now runs along the southern edge of the field, and ¼ mile brings you to the lean-to and the bluff overlooking Streeter Lake. Here you can camp for the night.

Second Day

From Streeter Lake Lean-to to Bassetts Creek
Distance: 3.8 miles
Hiking time: 2 hours

For your second day's hike, follow the road immediately behind the lean-to south as it passes Streeter Lake and then swings around to the southern side of the lake. Here a road intersects on the right that leads to a small Shuler family cemetery.

The main road, however, continues south past Crystal Lake to where another road intersects on the right; this 0.4 mile-long road takes you along the southern edge of the lake. The main trail continues southward, crossing a small brook feeding into Tamarack Creek located a short distance to the east; ½ mile further brings you to a road intersecting on the left. This road runs parallel to the one you are now walking for 1½ miles, and then swings west to rejoin it again, thereby forming a loop. To the east of this road is a peaked mountain, Francis Hill (el. 1,836 feet).

Bear to the right, and continue on the main route; ¼ mile brings you to the Middle Branch of the Oswegatchie River. The road turns left and follows the river for a little over ¼ mile, where it turns right and heads due south. A mile further brings you to the intersection with the parallel road mentioned earlier. A short distance beyond the fork, the trail crosses a wooden bridge over Bassetts Creek, named after the land's earlier owner who had a deer hunting camp here.

A short distance beyond the bridge, the trail ends at an old circular log landing area. Originally the trial ran south all the way to the Herkimer County line; only bushwhacking with map and compass would allow you to reach this point now. From here you can retrace your steps, all the while enjoying this rare access to the headwaters of the Oswegatchie River and some of the densest wilderness in the north country.

Greenwood Creek State Forest

Total distance: 7½ miles
Hiking time: 3 hours
Vertical rise: 280 feet
Map: USGS 7½' Fine; DEC Pamphlet with map

Greenwood Creek is not all that unusual a name, but it does have an appealing ring to it, and Greenwood seems to fit this small parcel of state real estate sitting adjacent to the Adirondack Forest Preserve. Appealing serves to describe everything about this state forest—the several stands of tall, well-spaced red pines, the attractive mix of birches and maples, the assortment of hiking trails, the picnic area, and above all the waterfall where Greenwood Creek tumbles down through huge boulders.

The state forest encompasses just 1,009 acres spreading over an area two miles wide by two miles long. Yet by the time you have walked all the footpaths, lanes, and roads, and returned to your starting point, you'll have covered more than seven miles—a good day's hike.

Flowing through the northern portion of the state forest is a small, cool stream, Greenwood Creek, which rises several miles to the east deep in the unpopulated Adirondack Park region. It meanders through the state forest, turns north, and eventually empties into Big Creek, a short distance from East Pitcairn.

The creek gives a good account of itself in the state forest, especially at the picnic site. Here you find a cluster of boulders piled on each other as if some giant had left a huge rock pile. Spilling over the boulders is Greenwood Creek, sparkling in the sunlight and splashing from rock to rock into a wide, clear pool. It's the perfect picnic spot.

Greenwood Creek State Forest is on the southwest boundary of St. Lawrence County, halfway between Harrisville and Fine on NY 3. Here you have entered the remoteness of the western Adirondacks, with its sparse population, few roads, and endless tracts of forest.

Access. Greenwood Creek State Forest is reached easily by NY 3 from Watertown, about 40 miles to the west. Traveling east from Watertown, NY 3 brings you to Harrisville and then to Pitcairn. From Pitcairn, continue east for 5.4 miles, where a dirt road marked by a sign to Greenwood Creek State Forest intersects from the right. Turn here, and drive 1.2 miles south; this will take you across Greenwood Creek and to the picnic area. Park here.

Trail. There is only one foot-trail in the state forest. It is a 1.8 mile loop trail that begins and ends at the picnic area. The rest of your hiking is on hard-surfaced dirt roads and several lanes that serve as truck trails. All are shaded to make walking a pleasure even on a hot, sunny day.

Start your hike by following the trail markers up along the edge of the falls at the picnic area. As you reach the top of this little hill, the trail turns right and heads uphill into the woods. After a short but steady climb, you make a short, gradual descent to the edge of Greenwood Creek.

The trail runs on the level for a short stretch and then begins to move up the slope of a hill; a 50-foot climb brings you to the top where the terrain levels out. You are surrounded here by tall red pines that create a most inviting forest setting—not too open, not too overgrown.

Soon you come to a dirt road. Turn left here, and follow the road as it heads east for a little over ¼ mile where it turns south. A ½ mile more brings you to a gate with a stop sign that marks the boundary of the state forest; beyond is private land. Retrace your steps to the intersection with the foot-trail you hiked earlier.

Pass by the foot-trail, and continue west of the dirt road as it heads downhill. A short walk brings you to a one-lane dirt road intersecting from the left. Turn here and head southwest. The terrain in this part of the state forest is flat. As you walk, you will be passing again through stands of red pine and then stands of hardwood, mostly maple and birch. A mile brings you to another gate with a stop sign marking the southern edge of the state forest. Retrace your steps to the main dirt road.

Turn left onto the dirt road, and continue walking westward. After 0.2 mile, the road turns north. At this bend, a lane intersects on the left, where discs nailed to trees mark this as a winter snowmobile trail. Turn onto this trail and head west.

The terrain in this section is a little more varied and rolling, which makes your hike even more enjoyable as you

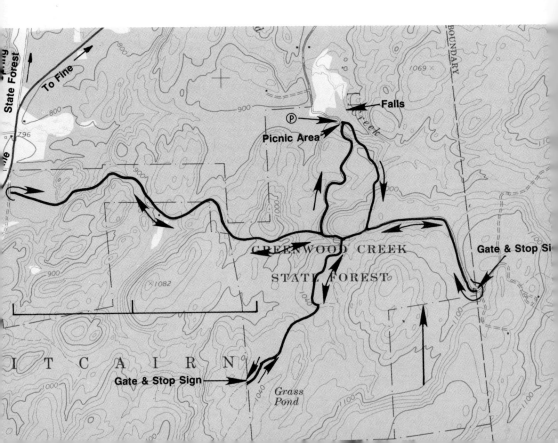

Greenwood Creek falls in Greenwood Creek State Forest

walk in the cool shade. The trail loops first to the right and then to the left, and at the mile mark it crosses a small brook. In the next ½ mile, the trail makes a gradual descent and levels out just before intersecting a north-south lane. Turn right onto this lane, and a few steps bring you to NY 3.

Retrace your steps to the main dirt road. Turn left onto it as it heads north. This section of the road wiggles a bit, making short turns to the right and then to the left as it heads gradually downhill.

In a little less than ½ mile, you are back at the picnic area and your parked vehicle.

Camping is not permitted at the picnic area, but there are many other spots in the state forest where it is. You can combine your hike here with a short one at Cold Spring Brook State Forest if you want a full day of hiking, or if you would like to spend a weekend in the area. Cold Spring Brook State Forest (see Hike 44) is a scant two miles north of East Pitcairn.

Cold Spring Brook State Forest

Total distance: 3½ miles
Hiking time: 1½ hours
Vertical Rise: 309 feet
Maps: USGS 7½' Fine; USGS 7½' Harrisville

This elongated parcel of state land is ideal for a short day trip. Hiking here can be combined with some in Greenwood Creek State Forest (see Hike 43), just two miles to the south, and with Toothaker State Forest to the southwest to make either a full day of walking or a weekend backpacking trip.

As is generally the case in these parts, the terrain of Cold Spring Brook State Forest is relatively level, although from Cold Spring Brook in the eastern sector to the road's end in the southwestern sector the land rises gradually 250 feet to reach the highest elevation in the state forest at 1,109 feet.

In the eastern end of the state forest, a low marshy area with pond-like characteristics is produced by the water of Cold Spring Creek. Here too is the half-mile long Big Pine Nature Trail, which, as its name indicates, runs through a stand of tall white pines.

One dirt road traverses almost the entire state forest, giving you access to Mud Pond and Toothaker Creek in the eastern half and, if you want to do some route finding by compass, to a jeep trail running southwest 2½ miles past Bullhead Pond to Toothaker State Forest. Several jeep trails run throughout hilly Toothaker State Forest (which your topo map identifies as Cooper Hill).

When you hike Cold Spring Brook State Forest, look about carefully. The terrain is representative of this region's physiographic and topographic charcteristics. Geologically, the state forest lies in what is called the Adirondack Mountains province, which in turn is subdivided into the highlands on the eastern boundary of the Adirondack region and the lowlands in the northwestern section. The Adirondack lowlands are really the foothills of the higher eastern mountains. The hills are low, the forest is dense, and there are many swampy wetlands. Instead of valleys, one finds shallow, wet depressions separated by low ridges of hard rock. The courses of such waterways as the Oswegatchie River snake back and forth in a most tortuous manner.

This area also is part of the Grenville Province of the Canadian Shield, to which the Adirondack Mountains are connected by a narrow neck in the Thousand Islands region called the Frontenac Axis. The rocks here are made almost entirely of Grenville-age crystalline material. They are over 1,100 million years old, going back to a time when the Adirondacks were as high as the Himalayas.

There are important differences between the rocks in the lowlands and the highlands. The lowland rocks are made up mainly of metasedimentary material derived from shales, limestones, and sandstones and from metavolcanic material. The highland rocks are made of metamorphosed igneous intrusive material to yield granites, syenites, and anorthosites.

The line separating these two physiographically different regions passes through Natural Bridge, Harrisville, and Pierrepont. Cold Spring Brook State Forest sits on this geologically abrupt, and puzzling, dividing line.

Access. The state forest can be reached by NY 3 from Watertown, which lies 40 miles to the west. Follow NY 3 east from Watertown past Harrisville to Pitcairn. From Pitcairn, drive 3.6 miles east on NY 3 to a road intersecting on the left. A sign directs you to East Pitcairn. Take this road, and drive 2.6 miles north to a dirt road intersecting on the left. (The land you have passed on the west side of the road is part of the state forest.) Turn here, and drive 0.2 mile to a sign indicating the start of the Big Pine Nature Trail on your right. Park here.

Trail. The Big Pine Nature Trail, while short, is a delight to walk. It winds its way through a stand of impressively large pine trees. The trail follows the east side of Cold Spring Creek and eventually ends at the northern boundary of the

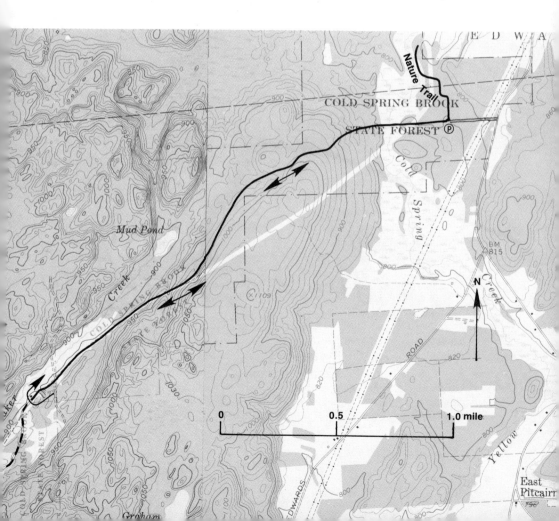

Hiker crossing footbridge on Big Pine Nature Trail in Cold Spring Brook State Forest

state forest. After the half-mile hike, retrace your steps to your parked vehicle, where you turn right onto the main dirt road and head west. A little over ¼ mile brings you to a watery, swampy section through which Cold Spring Creek flows. This is a good feeding, resting, and breeding area for waterfowl. On a given day, you may see ducks resting on the water or taking to flight at your approach.

The elevation here is 800 feet. Once past the creek, the road begins to rise gently as it runs west and then southwest in the next mile. You have now reached an elevation of 1,000 feet. The land on your left continues to rise, topping out at

a knob at 1,109 feet. A little further to the south, there is another knob with an elevation of 1,080 feet.

The road now begins to pitch gradually downward. On the right, the land slopes down to Mud Pond, the source of Toothaker Creek, which flows southwest to and through the middle of Toothaker State Forest.

Another mile brings you to road's end and a turn-around area. If you are adventuresome, you can take map and compass and bushwhack to the lane that leads to Toothaker State Forest. If you do not want to try the exercise, retrace your steps to your vehicle.

Wolf Lake State Forest

Total distance: 4.6 miles
Hiking time: 3 hours
Vertical rise: 1,120 feet
Maps: USGS 7½' Edwards; USGS 7½' Bigelow

This is outcrop country, where you find huge slabs of exposed rock that have been rounded and polished by the scrubbing action of glaciers as they crunched their way south into New York several times during the Pleistocene epoch. Technically, such bedrock outcrops are called *roche moutonnée* (from the French meaning "fleecy rock"), but more popularly they are referred to as "sheepbacks."

This is also talc country. Talc is usually formed when magnesium-rich rocks are altered, especially with heated water, and it is found in irregular deposits in metamorphic rocks along with serpentine, chlorite schists, and dolomite. Talc is used for talcum powder and paint fillers. It may be granular, fibrous, or soft, with a color between dull white to dark gray. At one time there were several talc mines near Talcville, and collecting sites of the mine dumps of the former United States Talc Company are found just a short distance west of town.

Geologically, the land belongs to the Adirondack Mountain Province, a small part of the much larger Grenville Province of the Canadian Shield, which extends south by a narrow neck under the St. Lawrence River by the Thousand Islands Bridge. Hence, you are encountering some very old rocks, indeed. Adirondack rocks originated over 1,100 million years ago.

When the Adirondacks were created, they resembled the modern Himalayas. Over eons of time, they have been worn down to their present size, and in the Western Adirondacks today the land is in low relief, with low ridges and shallow depressions and a terrain that is uneven and accented by boggy wetlands. The 4,315-acre Wolf Lake State Forest, near the southwestern edge of St. Lawrence County, falls into what is called the Adirondack Lowlands. Here are found marble, syenite, and paragneiss rocks. Students of mineralogy know that St. Lawrence County is internationally famous for mineral collecting. The area in and around Wolf Lake State Forest is no exception.

Many of the depressions in this area are long and deep, resulting in rock-encircled lakes. Three beautiful examples occur in the state forest— Huckleberry Lake, Wolf Lake, and Moon Lake. The lakes are the real treat of this hike: rock-bound, graced by evergreens, and sparkling in the sunlight. Near each is a lean-to, so it is easy to stay a few days.

There are just over ten miles of hiking trails in the state forest. All are groomed

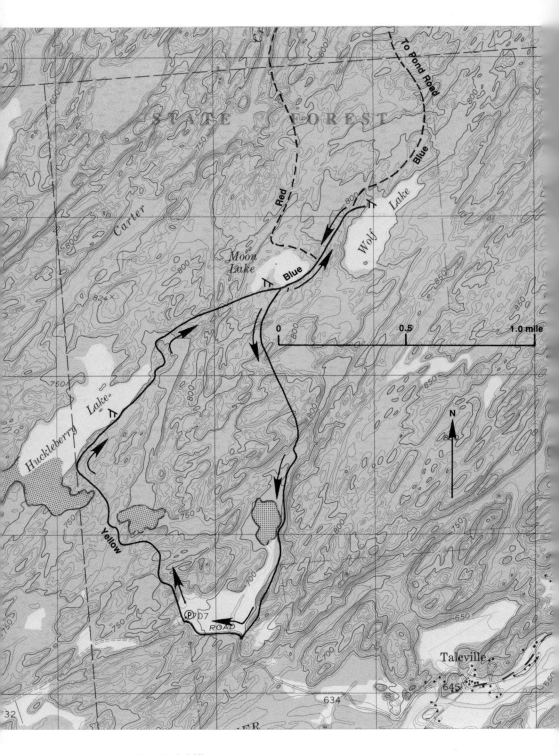

and marked, with trailheads at both the south and north ends of the state forest.

Access. Wolf Lake is reached via NY 58, which runs between Gouveneur in the north and Fine (near NY 3) in the south. If you are coming from Fine, you see at the eight-mile mark a sign directing you to the hamlet of Edwards. From this sign continue on NY 58 for 3.6 miles where you see a blacktop road intersecting on the right. Coming from Gouveneur, 8.5 miles bring you to a bridge crossing the West Branch of the Oswegatchie River. From the bridge, continue on NY 58 for 2.6 miles to the intersection of the blacktop road on your left.

Here a sign directs you to Talcville. A mile takes you to a bridge over the Oswegatchie River at the southern edge of the hamlet. Beyond the bridge, half a city block length brings you to a dirt road intersecting on the left. Turn here, and follow this dirt road for 1.2 miles, where it makes a 90-degree turn to the left. At this bend is the beginning of Moon Lake Trail. From here, continue for another ¼ mile down the road to a fairly large parking area where the Huckleberry Lake Trail begins. Park here.

Those interested in mineral collecting should look for the collecting site a short distance after turning onto the dirt road in Talcville. Drive a little over 0.2 mile on the dirt road; after crossing the railroad tracks for the third time, you will see mining dumps on the left side, between the tracks and the river.

Here a whole talc deposit suite of minerals can be found: talc, hexagonite, wollastonite, serpentine, phlogopite, scapolite, diopside, pyrite, calcite, and various forms of tremolite, some of which fluoresce. Hexagonite is a rare manganese-bearing species of tremolite, with a distinctive lavender color. The unusual species for this area is groutite, a

hydrous manganese oxide that takes the form of small lustrous black crystals.

Trail. Topographically, the land here is relatively flat, with the highest elevation being only 850 feet. When you are hiking, however, you find that you go forever up and down as the trail snakes its way through, over, and around the numerous large rock outcrops.

To get started is a bit of a challenge. The grass grows high in summer and almost obscures the entrance, but you soon pick up the signs of a discernible foot-trail that you can follow north through the grass for about 100 yards. Here you see a post with a yellow trail marker. Another 50 yards bring you into the woods and onto a wide, well-used trail. As all the trail markers are yellow, we can refer to the Huckleberry Lake Trail as the Yellow Trail.

It is a mile via the Yellow Trail to Huckleberry Lake. Once on the trail, a short distance into the forest you pass between two large outcrops, a sample of the rocky landscape you'll encounter for the rest of your hike. The area is heavily wooded, predominantly maple with a generous sprinkling of white birch trees to make this a picturesque forest.

At the ½-mile mark, you see a body of water on your right through the woods, a pond filled with dead trees, the result of water backed up by a beaver dam. A ¼ mile further, the water that you see on your left is the low swampy southern end of Huckleberry Lake.

In less than ¼ mile, you climb onto a smooth rock bluff, and ahead of you is beautiful Huckleberry Lake, complete with several rounded, glacier-scoured islands, where small shrubs and a few pine trees have been able to find a foothold.

The trail now runs on the bluff along the side of the lake. Brush-wide yellow stripes are painted on the rocks to keep you on course. A ¼ mile brings you to a lean-to on a rock slab at the lake's edge.

In the next ¼ mile, the trail swings a little to the right and away from the lake until you are no longer able to see it. At another depression filled with water and dead trees on the right, the trail swings to the left, climbs a small hill, and descends to a log footbridge over the bog's narrow north end.

From here, it is ½ mile over even more smooth, rocky terrain to Moon Lake. You will see a lean-to as the trail circles the southern portion of the lake. A short distance uptrail from the lean-to, the Moon Lake Trail intersects on the right. This is the trail you'll take on your return.

The trail markers now change from yellow to blue. Continue in a northerly direction by following the blue markers. In a little less than ¼ mile, you come to another trail intersection. A sign here directs you to Wolf Lake toward the right and "Beaver Ponds Trail and Podunk" to the left. The Beaver Ponds Trail is 2.8 miles long and marked with red; at the two-mile mark is a lean-to.

Continue northeast, though, on the backs of the smooth rocks and following the blue markers, for the next ¼ mile. On your right you see the water of Wolf Lake, and then the trail turns to the right and takes you a short distance to a lean-to on the lake's edge. This lake, like the other two, is rock-encircled and equally attractive.

From the lean-to, the Blue Trail runs 2.4 miles north, ending at Pond Road. To complete your southern loop, however, retrace your steps to the Moon Lake Trail, and turn left. The markers you find here initially are blue, but a short distance downtrail yellow markers appear, which soon give way to red and then blue paint on trees, with the yellow markers reappearing near the end.

This trail is a bit more hilly and not quite as attractive as the Yellow Trail. At the ½-mile mark, you come to a narrow, V-shaped depression filled with water and dead trees. The trail weaves its way through rocks and boulders along the pond, and up ahead you see several beaver dams.

The log footbridge takes you over the outlet stream and then along the side of a long ridge, which, while not too high, nonetheless has steep sides. A little over ¼ mile brings you to still another fairly large beaver pond. The trail skirts the eastern edge and climbs higher up the hill. In little under ½ mile, you exit from the forest onto the dirt road over which you drove before. Turn right to follow the road west, past the open, field-like area, over the outlet stream and back to your parked vehicle.

Frank E. Jadwin Memorial Forest

Total distance: 11.2 miles (two days)
Hiking time: 6 hours
Vertical rise: 520 feet
Maps: USGS 7½′ Natural Bridge; USGS 7½′ Remington
  Corners

Too much of a good thing, someone once remarked, is wonderful. While that may be true in the case of Frank E. Jadwin Memorial Forest, it is also something of a challenge. The challenge is to determine just what section of this large state forest to hike; it is hard to decide what options to take.

Jadwin is immense. At 19,964 acres, 10 miles wide and 14 miles long, it is one of the largest state forests in upstate New York. Yet it is easy to reach from either NY 3, which runs along its northern boundary, or NY 812, which runs south from NY 3 through the state forest's central portion.

While there is no designated hiking trail in Jadwin Forest, a network of dirt roads, truck trails, and jeep trails allows the hiker to design a route of almost any length. These roads let you reach, explore, and—if you brought your angling gear—fish the upper portions of two rivers. Indian River runs along the western boundary. The West Branch of the Oswegatchie River runs through the entire length of the state forest, with several bridge crossings and fishing accesses.

In general, the state forest, like so much Western Adirondack land, is relatively flat and thickly forested. Creeks and rivers drain to the north and west. The terrain is characterized by low, irregular ridges and numerous depressions with swampy areas or water routes of the slow-moving creeks and rivers.

Geologically, Jadwin lies close to the boundary between the two sections of the Adirondacks, the highlands and the lowlands. This line runs through Natural Bridge, Harrisville, and Pierrepont, a short distance north of the state forest. The difference between the two regions is found in their rock formations. The highlands are underlain by metamorphosed igneous rock, while the lowlands are underlain by interlayered metamorphosed sedimentary and volcanic rock.

In this regard, Jadwin Forest is part of the highland region, while its close neighbor, Onjebonge State Forest (see Hike 47), less than a mile to the north, lies on the other side of the boundary in the lowland region. Topographically, of course, there is little difference between the two forests.

Jadwin's western portion between the Indian River and the West Branch of the Oswegatchie is flatter and lower (el. 850 feet) than the eastern portion, where the terrain is irregular and higher, rising to 1,200 feet.

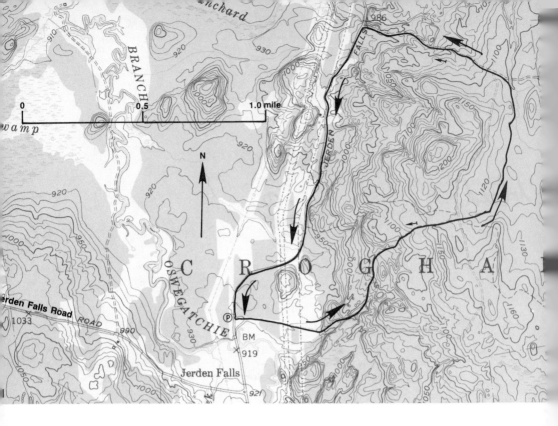

To get a feel for the variety in this state forest, it is best to see it in two stages, hiking a section in the northwestern part and one in the southwestern part, so you should plan a weekend trip. Either section could serve as a one-day hike, of course.

Access. The trail head for the first day's hike can be reached from NY 3, which runs east from Watertown. From Natural Bridge, drive 1.2 miles until the road crosses a railroad track. On the other side, old NY 3 forks to the right. Take this fork, and drive 1.2 miles to the intersection with Henry Road. Turn right here, and follow Henry Road past Blanchard Pond to its intersection with Factory Road. Turn right onto Factory Road, and follow it for a mile, where a single-lane dirt truck trail, Aldrich Road, intersects on the left. Park here.

First Day

Factory Road to Indian River Flats
Distance: 7.2 miles
Hiking time: 4 hours

The road to Indian River Flats in the south runs on flat terrain with a vertical rise of less than 100 feet, a rise that is hardly noticeable during your hike. You are moving through a heavily forested area, and most of the time the road is shaded. The road heads in a southeasterly direction for the first 11.4 miles, at which point another single-lane truck trail, Patchin Road, intersects on the left.

Continue south on Aldrich Road for another 0.2 mile where you see a house on the left (marked by a sign reading "Whippoorwill Ridge") on a small triangular piece of private land whose point touches the road. Continuing for another 0.3 mile, you see an abandoned building on your left, and 0.4 mile further brings you to an intersection with another truck trail, Nelson Road.

Continue past Nelson Road. Aldrich Road swings more sharply southward and then turns southwesterly. In 0.4 mile, you reach a truck trail, Wahalula Road, that intersects on the left. At this point, Aldrich Road turns to the right, and a short distance beyond a narrow lane

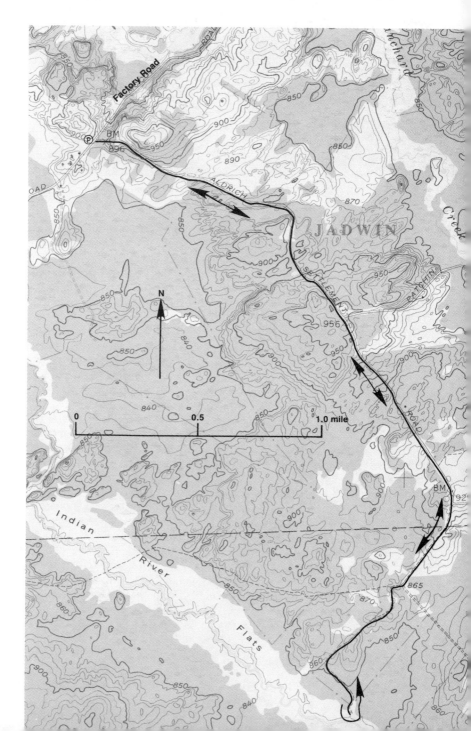

Indian River flowing along southern edge of Jadwin Memorial Forest

forks to the right.

Stay on Aldrich Road as it turns sharply to the south; 0.8 mile brings you to the road's end at Indian River and an open, flat area called Indian Flats. Here you can take time to study the landscape while enjoying your lunch before retracing your steps to your vehicle.

Second Day

Jerden Falls Road via Truck Trail back to Jerden Falls Road
Distance: 4 miles
Hiking time: 2 hours

To reach the trailhead for your second day, drive back to NY 3 via Henry Road. Where Henry Road intersects the old NY 3, turn right; in 0.4 mile you come to the present-day NY 3. Turn right onto NY 3, and drive 5.8 miles to NY 812, which intersects on the right. Turn here, and drive south on NY 812 for 7.8 miles, where Jerden Falls Road intersects on the left. Turn onto Jerden Falls Road, and follow it for two miles until it turns to the left and crosses the West Branch of the Oswegatchie River; 0.1 mile on the

north side of the river, you see a single-lane truck trail that goes off to the right. Park here.

The truck trail makes a loop that will bring you back to your start. At the outset, the road is flat for the first 0.4 mile; en route you walk under powerlines running in a north-south direction. Beyond the powerlines, the terrain begins to slope upward. For the next mile you continue a steady, albeit gradual, uphill climb to an elevation of 1,130 feet (200 feet vertical rise).

Before reaching a level area, you have a nice view to the west overlooking the West Branch of the Oswegatchie River. The land now levels out, and for the next half-mile the road runs over flat terrain. At the 1.8-mile mark, the road touches the western edge of Blanchard Creek. Here the road turns westerly and starts a gradual descent. A downhill walk of 0.8 mile brings you to Jerden Falls Road, where the west-flowing Blanchard Creek crosses under it. Turn left on Jerden Falls Road, and walk south on this dirt road back to your vehicle 1.4 miles away.

Onjebonge and Hogsback State Forests

Total distance: 8 miles
Hiking time: 4 hours
Vertical rise: 810 feet
Map: USGS 7½′ Natural Bridge

Onjebonge State Forest and Hogsback State Forest, as close neighbors, are ideal for a day's trek in an area typical of the forested Western Adirondacks. Amateur geologists will find many rocks worth studying and minerals worth collecting nearby.

Both state forests are easy to reach via NY 3. Terrain in both is relatively flat for easy walking. Both have roads or trails running their entire length. The 624-acre Hogsback State Forest, a mile northeast of Onjebonge, is four miles east of Natural Bridge. Onjebonge lies a little over ½ mile north of Natural Bridge (so named because a branch of the Indian River disappears just north of the village, runs underground for about 0.1 mile, and then emerges to rejoin the river's main branch). Crossing the river at this point, you are driving over a "natural bridge," one of the many geological phenomena you find in this region.

The western edge of the 1,826-acre Onjebonge State Forest lies on the Lewis-Jefferson County line. This also is the abrupt geological boundary separating the Adirondack lowlands from the Adirondack highlands, which runs northeasterly through Natural Bridge, Harrisville, and Pierrepont. To the north and west of this line are found underlying rocks making up the lowland region; to the south and east are a different set of rocks that makes up the highland region.

Specifically, the highlands are underlain by metamorphosed igneous intrusive rocks such as granite, charnockite, syenite, gabbre, and anorthosite. In contrast, the lowland Adirondacks are mainly underlain by interlayered metamorphosed sedimentary and volcanic rocks that are tightly and plastically folded.

All the features characterizing the Adirondack lowlands are found in Onjebonge. Over eons of time, erosion has produced a surface of low ridges of gneiss rock with intervening marshy low areas underlain by marble. All through the state forest, there are low outcrops, rounded and smoothed by the scouring action of advancing glaciers, four of which moved over New York during the Pleistocene epoch. Also found here are erratics, boulders from another region that were brought south with an advancing glacier and left behind when the glacier melted back.

Hogsback State Forest lies on the other side of the geological boundary in the highlands region. En route to it, you can stop to do some exploring for

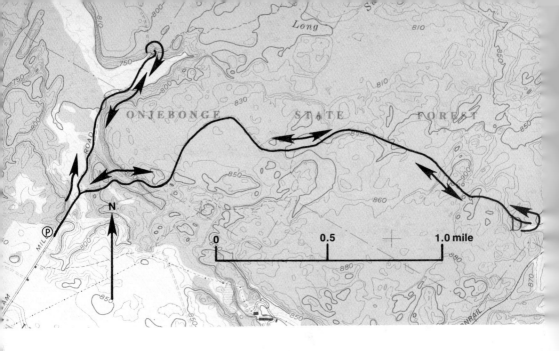

minerals at a famous old Dana collecting site, just off NY 3 when you drive east from Natural Bridge. (From the center of the village, drive 1.2 miles to where a dirt road intersects on the right. The collecting site consists of trenches about 75 yards into the field on the right side of the highway and the right side of the dirt road.) Mineralization has occurred here in marble-filled fissures in a syenitic gneiss. Crystals at this site are small but exceptionally well-formed. You can find individual crystals or aggregates of all combinations of apatite, pyroxene, scapelite, titanite, wollastonite, and zircon.

The thickly forested terrain of the state forests is not well drained because of the underlying Precambrian rock. There are many swampy areas throughout Onjebonge; Long Swamp in the north is the largest. Hogsback differs a bit, containing instead two small ponds, Fitzgerald and Hogsback Ponds. Several small streams that eventually reach Indian River (which touches the western part of Onjebonge) rise in each state forest.

One road takes you through Hogsback

State Forest. Onjebonge has a truck trail with a number of jeep trails radiating off it. All can be hiked and explored, but you'll need map and compass to find and follow the unmarked Onjebonge trails, which together can add another ten miles to your hike. One of these trails connects with a KOA campground a little over a mile south of the state forest.

Access. Onjebonge can be reached via NY 3, which runs east out of Watertown. From Watertown, it is about 24 miles to Natural Bridge, where in the center of the hamlet you encounter an intersection. Turn left (north) here. This road crosses the "natural bridge" and then a bridge over the east branch of Indian River. Once over the latter bridge, you immediately turn left onto River Road, and drive north for 0.4 mile where a dirt road, Steam Mill Road, intersects on the right. Turn here, and drive for 0.4 mile; this brings you into the state forest. Park here.

Trail. There are no marked hiking trails